Inventory and
Production Decisions

Research in Business Economics and Public Policy, No. 7

Fred Bateman, Series Editor

Chairman and Professor
Business Economics and Public Policy
Indiana University

Other Titles in This Series

Inventory and Production Decisions

by
Mansfield W. Williams

UMI RESEARCH PRESS
Ann Arbor, Michigan

Produced and distributed by
UMI Research Press
an imprint of
University Microfilms International
A Xerox Information Resources Company
Ann Arbor, Michigan 48106

Library of Congress Cataloging in Publication Data

Williams, Mansfield W. (Mansfield Wiggin)
Inventory and production decisions.

(Research in business economics and public policy ;
no. 7)
Revision of thesis (Ph. D.)–Rutgers Unviersity, 1981,
which had title: Manufacturers' decisions on production
and inventory levels.
Bibliography: p.
Includes index.
1. Inventory control–Mathematical models.
2. Production control–Mathematical models. I. Title.
II. Series.

HD40.W54 1984   658.7'87'0724   83-18179
ISBN 0-8357-1446-2

Contents

List of Tables

List of Figures

Acknowledgments

Appreciation is due to many for their careful review and helpful criticism, in particular to Prof. Hiroki Tsurumi. Throughout this study, his contributions and guidance have been invaluable. His ability to ask the stimulating question, rather than providing the easy answer, coupled with constant encouragement, have been in the best Socratic tradition.

Every study has its starting point. I am indebted to the work of Dr. David A. Belsley on the distinction between production to stock and production to order, and the analytical approach he developed.

My greatest debt is to the 100 percent support of my family. My dear wife, Peggy, has been solid gold. And the competition provided by two current doctoral candidates, Chip and Laurie, has undoubtedly been a factor in their father's early completion of this study.

1

Introduction

Production is one of the basic functions underlying economic activity, and the literature on the subject is correspondingly voluminous. Inventories, which are concomitant to production, have received a generous, though smaller degree of attention. Nevertheless:

> Obscurities, ambiguities, and errors exist in cost and supply analysis despite, or because of, the immense literature on the subject. Especially obscure are the relationships between cost and output, both in the long run and in the short run.[1]

How manufacturers determine "how much currently to produce, and of which products," in the short term, is addressed by this study. Manufacturers also hold inventories, and the question of "how much should be held" will be examined. Whether, and how well, profit-maximizing principles provide answers to these questions is an integral part of the analysis.

Microtheory provides the obvious starting point toward answer of these questions. Since the microeconomic theory of the firm is essentially an equilibrium concept, a logical preliminary would be to enquire how disequilibrium in the market becomes equilibrium. Actually, there are two explanations, derived from opposite sides of the English Channel (figure 1).

Marshall viwed the disequilibrium as one in which a difference existed between p^S and p^D, given the quantity of product available in a particular market. The signal to producers for the quantity adjustment required to equilibrium, $\overset{o}{q}$, came through adjustment of the market price to a different level (i.e., price adjustment leads q). In the Walrasian explanation, there is a starting difference in quantities supplied and demanded at (existing)[2] market price. Adjustment of these quantities leads to price adjustment at an equilibrium level. In the "General Theory," Keynes utilized the Walrasian approach to explain[3] sticky behavior of prices (at least downward), and the signal to producers that a change in output was in order came through unexpected changes in inventory (i.e., the latter providing the initial quantity adjustment required).

Figure 1.   Marshallian and Walrasian Disequilibrium;
Initial Positions

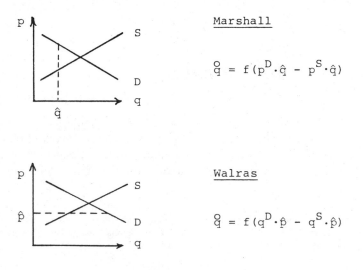

Where: p and q denote price and quantity. Superscripts
(D) and (S) relate to the pertinent schedule, and the
superscript (^) to the initially observed (disequilibrium)
p or q. $\overset{o}{q}$ = final equilibrium q.

In equilibrium, microtheory of the firm provides[4] the profit-maximizing
rule for a perfectly competitive manufacturer of a single product, that:

$$MC = P. \tag{1.1}$$

In other words, the manufacturer's task, to maximize profit, is to equate price
and marginal cost. When the firm's activities are extended to embrace a
production process with multiple outputs and inputs, the profit-maximizing
rules may be generalized to a triad of relations:[5]

$$\frac{p_j}{p_k} = -\frac{\partial q_k}{\partial q_j} \tag{1.2}$$

which says that the ratio at which output of one product should be exchanged
for another (or, the rate of product transformation) must equal the ratio of
their prices.

$$\frac{r_j}{r_k} = - \frac{\partial x_k}{\partial x_j} \tag{1.3}$$

which says that the ratio at which we would use input (j) in place of input (k) at the margin (or, the rate of technical substitution) will depend on their cost ratio.

$$r_j = \frac{\partial q_k}{\partial x_j} \cdot p_k' \tag{1.4}$$

which says that each input cost should be equated to the value of the marginal product of each input, where r_j = price of input x_j, p_j = selling price of the jth product, and q_j = quantity of the jth product.

Since producers have been relieved of uncertainty[6] about the demand facing their product(s), holdings of inventory have not been a (necessary) part of the development of these relations.

While unquestionably valuable in concept, and highly useful for expository purposes, the profit-maximizing rule (1.1), and its multi-product counterparts, suffer from some practical shortcomings. Perhaps this can best be illustrated by the following (hypothetical) assignment from the president of a typical multi-product firm (e.g., products numbered in the hundreds or thousands)[7] to the comptroller,

> Jones, our profit picture is anemic, and I'm concerned that our product-line managers are not maximizing profits. Prepare an analysis for me that will show whether each of our products is being sold currently at profit-maximizing levels, and what the volume to be sold during the next quarter should be to maximize profits.

Conceptually, the task is feasible, but if Jones fully realizes the difficulty of the assignment, there is little doubt that he would point out some of the problems in his path. Let us consider only two for the moment:

1. Marginal cost, while valuable as an economic concept, is not ordinarily available per se from standard cost-accounting records. Problems exist, including interdependence of processes, and the need for allocation of many cost elements between products. In practice, of course, costs are allocated, though by coincidence only, in consonance with marginal cost concepts.

2. The firm's experience is that the rate at which orders do/will come in is stochastic (i.e., uncertain and uneven).

Together, these propositions give rise to a second generation of considerations:

1. What will be the effects of stochastic demand on market price and short period sales volume? How will changes of P affect MC = P as an indicator of profit-maximizing volume?

   For purposes of mathematical treatment, stochastic demand is often presented as being "known up to a density function." But, of course, if one knew *that* well what to expect, the problem would be substantially ameliorated.

2. A firm knowing its "conventional costs" (e.g., average variable costs, standard volume costs, and normal effects of volume variances on standard cost), but not knowing MC, might be able to "more or less" approximate it. Are approximations valid?

   For example, would linear approximation in the relevant range undermine the convexity assumptions required for second order conditions?

3. If (by approximation) the MC's were judged to be fairly flat over the range relevant to decision, it is obvious that relatively small price changes would necessarily indicate fairly large changes be made in production level.

   For processes with little or no cost attached to changing levels of production, no difficulty would be posed. However, where such costs were significant, it would appear likely that very much in the way of changes would add to costs. Would adoption of such a policy actually be consistent with the profit-maximizing principle being addressed?

4. Of course, inventories of finished goods could be used to buffer changes in demand. But, how inventory costs (including opportunity costs of several types) relate to the propositions developed earlier is not at all clear.

   Practically speaking, firms have kept and will continue to keep inventories so that question does not relate to "whether to inventory?" but rather, how to incorporate the costs related to keeping inventories with marginal cost derivation and use.

   A quotation from the *Wall Street Journal* of August 15, 1980 is pertinent here (figure 2).

The 1973-1975 recession taught most American businessmen all they needed to know about inventory control. Or so, as late as last year, they thought. Despite all the attention inventory has got in the last five years, however, keeping just the right amount of goods on hand has proved neither simple nor painless.

Figure 2. Business Sales and Inventories, Seasonally
Adjusted, in Billions of Dollars

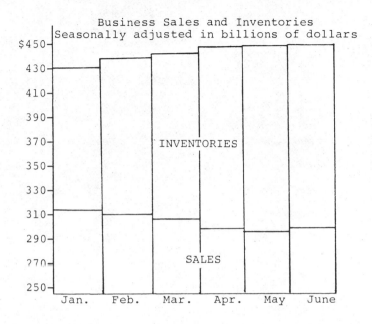

5. Jones might well wish to avoid the stigma of simply being negative, by making a positive suggestion. "Boss, I've got a great idea. If profit improvement is what we need, let's just set some appropriate profit targets[8] for each product line, and have the managers' bonuses depend on making them. They'll *do* it!!"

   Whether such an approach is indeed profit-maximizing is a valid question. However, the answer need not be an automatic negative. Let us consider the manager trying to maximize *his own* gains. Given the task above, he might best be able to accomplish the objective by, perhaps intuitively, using MC = P as a guideline. Wouldn't this qualify?

   Our pursuit of the example presented above does not say, of course, that profit-maximizing is not possible for a multi-product firm facing uncertain demand. It does, however, provide the thought that profit-maximizing via equations (1.1)–(1.4) will not be directly useful to a typical (multi-product) firm, or as Joskow[9] puts it, "... the traditional tools of the theory of the firm are not very helpful."

2

An Inventory of the Literature

Production and inventories of finished goods share a sibling relation. An output decision affects the amount which will be in inventory, and decision to adjust inventory size is accomplished by changing production rate. If the firm wishes to avoid changing the rate of output, inventory, by absorbing (or supplying) extra product, provides the necessary cushion or buffer. To put in perspective various ways in which production and inventory (either singly, or together) have been treated, this chapter will survey contributions to be found in the literature.

If typical firms operated under the conditions of perfect competition (including certainty), standard microtheory of the firm would provide most of the information needed. However, as demonstrated by the example addressed in the preceding chapter, firms face a broader array of questions in attempting to maximize profits under conditions of uncertainty. The coverage of topics in this chapter reflects this need.

For convenience, our samplings will be subdivided into four areas of broad definition: (1) classical writers, (2) microeconomics, (3) macroeconomics (including business cycle and econometric studies), and (4) industrial management and operations research.

Classical Writers

Edmund Cartwright invented the power loom in 1785, and the Industrial Revolution was in full stride by the early 1800s. Accordingly, it is no surprise that there were sound and perceptive views on manufacturing activities expressed in that era and later, although without the mathematical expression which is now so familiar.

In 1836 George Ramsay[1] was pointing out how the steps of production, distribution, exchange, and consumption were necessarily linked together, and John Stuart Mill's[2] 1844 observations on the difference between rapid circulation and stagnation of inventories is an apt description of the relation between inventories and business cycles. As Mill put it,

> There is a *brisk demand* and a rapid circulation, when goods, generally speaking, are sold as fast as they can be produced. There is *slackness,* on the contrary, and stagnation, when goods, which have been produced, remain for a long time unsold. In the former case, the capital which has been locked up in production is disengaged as soon as the production is completed; and can immediately be employed in further production. In the latter case, a large portion of the productive capital of the country is lying in temporary inactivity.

Noteworthy here is the relation of working capital to the productive activity—a coupling notable for its relative absence in more modern references.

And some years later, John Bates Clark[3] in speaking of the manner in which all goods produced become divided into the shares which individuals receive, explained, "The terms of the division that is actually made, however, are fixed as the production of the goods goes on: the goods are really apportioned in the making." The last phrase is really very apt to describe how the factors of production are rewarded according to their marginal productivity.

Perhaps too recent to be considered a classical writer (if the adjective is deemed to denote date of authorship, rather than magisterial caliber of the work), mention of John Maynard Keynes is allotted to this section.

Some writers today (e.g., Michael Evans)[4] think that "Keynes spent very little time discussing inventories." Possibly, this is because the word "inventories" occurs just once in the "General Theory"[5] (on p. 322), wherein he remarks that "it is becoming usual" to use this term in description of stocks of finished and unfinished goods. His reference to *stocks* are numerous, and for example, it is Keynesian theory that production increases when the signal is given of additional demand at existing prices, by the drawing down of stocks. Some other Keynesian references which are interesting in their relation to positions taken by more recent writers include:

1. On the balancing of current production with interest charges and timing of delivery of product. "As the rate of interest rises, the proportion of prospective consumer's demand for which it pays to produce today shrinks pari passu."[6]
2. Regarding the role of the working off of surplus stocks, during downward turns in the trade cycle as "negative investment, which is a further deterrent to employment."[7]
3. Regarding oscillations within the main movement of the trade cycle caused by fluctuation of stocks (rather than expressing the view that inventory surpluses are the dominating influence).[8]

Microeconomics

Microeconomics has not ignored inventory across the boards—there are a number of useful studies, which can be cited:

1. Sweezy[9] suggested that in imperfect market competition, oligopolists might well cut prices and curtail production at the beginning of a decline in demand. He observed that this might be particularly likely for commodity products of long process time—e.g., copper. This is an interesting example of linking inventory levels, prices, and business cycle.

2. Whitin[10] developed the familiar square root relation between an optimum purchase (or production) quantity vs. the costs of its being carried in inventory,

$$Q = [\frac{2 \cdot R \cdot S}{I}]^{1/2} \qquad (1.2)$$

    where R = yearly requirement, S = setup costs, and I = inventory cost/unit.

3. Modigliani has given the following reasons for the holding of finished goods inventories:[11] (a) to smooth production and/or enable production of optimum lot sizes, (b) to buffer fluctuations in demand, and (c) to take advantage of expected price changes.

4. Vernon Smith[12] investigated the effect of fluctuating (but known) demand upon a one-product firm which uses a fixed input (e.g., capital), and a current input (e.g., labor). According to (a) above, an inventory could be used to enable a constant level of production, but, if operating without inventory, the firm must adjust production level up or down to keep in step with demand.

Intuitively, in the latter case, one would expect over-capacity of the capital asset to exist. Smith goes on to show that, in addition to more of the fixed input being required, the process will also need a larger amount of the current input (for any level of output) than would be required to produce constant output with an optimal fixed input installation. In other words, satisfying a variable demand, by correspondingly varying output levels, leads to a greater cost (both real and social) in terms both of larger current input usage over a period, and in greater fixed investment.

The alternative to equipping the process to meet the occasional peak demands would be producing at a constant (or, at least, a less variable) rate, using inventory as a buffer. Would this not be a lower cost approach? The answer, in Smith's terms, is that cost is indeed reduced—up to the point where the marginal cost of holding a unit of output in inventory (until required) equals (or exceeds) the current cost of its production. This implies that we could view the variable production model as providing an opportunity cost yardstick for optimal inventory investment (vs. additional fixed investment) and for inventory carrying cost (vs. the cost of the additional use of the current input required in the variable case).

Once again, a highly useful model for expository purposes. We are shown that, at least partially, investment in inventory is a substitute for capital investment. However, application to circumstances of demand fluctuating on a nonregular *and* imperfectly known basis suggests that a deterministic solution is harder to realize, than when demand conditions are, in fact, known.

What is lacking so far, of course, are tools which can be used under conditions of uncertain demand. Or, as Marc Nerlove has commented,[13]

> It is something of a caricature of static economic theory to say it deals with a world in which there are no transactions costs, no irreversibilities, where information is costless, and where frictions have no place. But such a characterization is not misleading.

Nerlove goes on to say that the "new"[14] microeconomics is concerned largely with the implications of exactly such imperfections and frictions, but that so far, it presents a promising approach, more than a developed dynamic theory.

A particularly valuable contribution has been made by Mills.[15] He observed that one obvious reason for holding inventory derives from the uncertainty about demand, together with the loss of profit which would ensue (without inventory) if sales were foregone. And since it is costly to change the rate of production, another reason for holding inventory is as a buffer.

Mills used game theory (L.J. Savage), and linear cost expressions on a mini-max basis, to arrive at a production rule which specifies optimum strategy under conditions of uncertainty. The costs considered were the cost of production, plus carrying costs for finished goods inventory, plus the two costs indicated above. The result was a regression testable relation:

$$P_t = b_o + b_1 P_{t-1} + b^2 H_{t-1} + b_3 S_t, \qquad (2.1)$$

where P_t = optimal production level for the current period, S_t = current period sales, H_{t-1} = finished goods inventory at the end of the preceding period (i.e., at the start of this), and P_{t-1} = last period's production level. (Results from testing of this expression are examined later in this study.)

An important direction of effort has been provided by David Baron and others, who have analyzed behavior of the firm under stochastic demand conditions. Their results help considerably to bridge the gap between the static-equilibrium perfect competitor, and the price-setting imperfect competitor who is responding to demand uncertainty with an appropriate strategy.

Baron[16] presents, as one polar case, a "pricing strategy," in which the producer maintains a set price ($\hat{p}$), and output (q) is allowed to vary according to the conditional density of demand, $f(q/\hat{p})$. The firm's expected profits will be:

$$E(\pi) = \hat{p} \cdot E(q/\hat{p}) - E(C_q/\hat{p}), \qquad (2.2)$$

where C_q is the total cost of producing q. Baron shows that a *risk-averse* producer will tend to choose a lower $\hat{p}$ (i.e., not to "lose" sales) than would be optimal, and that this has a detrimental effect on expected profits.

To go a step or two further, in similar vein Leland[17] has demonstrated plausibly that increases in expected total revenue are accompanied by increasing risk. Holthausen[18] has studied the firm's decisions on *inputs*, as affected by uncertain demand and reports that input decisions are not affected for the competitive firm and for the quantity-setting imperfect competitor. However, the risk-averse firm which is a price-setting imperfect competitor will use an expected capital/labor ratio less than the efficient ratio.

Suddenly we find we have reached and crossed a watershed of sorts. The static equilibrium theory with which we started is based on perfect competition. Under conditions of demand uncertainty: (1) the firm is no longer able to act with certainty, which is one of the attributes of the perfect competitor, (2) and in reacting to uncertain demand *by setting either volume or price*, another significant change from "perfect competition" has arisen.

We conclude this portion with Baron's observation that "most firms tend to use the pricing strategy" or some variation of it. One such variation, the "Mill's strategy" specifically introduces the use of inventory for production smoothing purposes—yet another step away from the static equilibrium case, and closer to observed behavior.

Application of the principle of uncertainty has emerged as one of the promising directions for the new microeconomics. Demand uncertainty is not the *only* area of uncertainty for the firm, of course. One recent article[19] reports on the results of analysis of the effects of stochastic input prices, with the conclusion that they give an imperfect competitor greater financial incentive to inventory input stocks than would be the case for a perfectly competitive firm.

Another promising direction of research is represented by efforts to incorporate cash flow and other financial variables into study of the firm's behavior. Louis de Alessi comments (with respect to the firm's adjustment to a change in market conditions), "As Alchian and others have emphasized, however, the crucial concept is the *wealth* effect of the alternative strategies considered by the firm."[20]

To illustrate that interest in this direction is increasing, in a recent empirical investigation, Richard Caves et al.[21] examined inventories, excess production capacity, and liquid financial assets as buffer stocks, which partially complement and partially substitute for one another. Treatment of the first two as (imperfect) substitutes is not new, but inclusion of the latter stock is a departure from "standard."

We cannot say, of course, that the importance of financial assets, or stocks of capital for the firm is a new concept. In fact, it is timely to remember the importance given this aspect by the classical writers. For example, to quote John Stuart Mill,

> Suppose I have laid out all the money I possess in wages and tools, and that the article I produce is just completed: —will it be said that I have no capital? Certainly not. I have the same capital as before, perhaps a greater, but it is locked up as the expression is.
>
> All unsold goods constitute a part of the national capital and of the capital of the producer or dealer to whom they belong.[22]

It would seem then, there has been a full turn of the wheel.

At this point, a brief but illustrative detour is in order. In monetary theory, distinction is made between the *financial* and the *real* sectors of the economy.[23]

The financial sector deals with the demand for and supply of money, and their interaction which determines the rate(s) of interest. A simple expression for this would be:

$$i = f(R_e, Y), \tag{2.3}$$

where i = interest rates, Y = GNP = gross national income, and hence the demand for money, and R_e = effective reserves of banks, as the basis of money supply. The real sector sums up spending for all final goods and services in the economy:

$$Y = C + I + G, \tag{2.4}$$

where C = personal consumption, I = (real) investment, and G = government spending. Equilibrium for the economy is expressed by a solution jointly satisfying both relations.

One would expect a similar approach, coupling real and financial concepts, to have been used in development of the theory of the firm, but *surprisingly,* this has not been the case. In fact, to illustrate the degree to which the standard microtheory of the firm has focussed on the real (or flow) elements to the exclusion of financial sector elements, we suggest comparison of the quotation[24] below with the foregoing development.

> Given the entrepreneur's production function, cost equation, and expansion path function, his total cost can be expressed as a function of output level. In the short run, the cost of his fixed inputs must be paid, regardless of his output level. The first-order condition for profit maximization requires the entrepreneur to equate his marginal cost to the selling price of his output. The second-order condition requires that marginal cost be increasing. The entrepreneur is able to vary the levels of his fixed inputs in the long run and therefore is able to select a particular short-run cost function. His long run total cost function is the envelope of his alternative short-run total cost functions. Long-run profit maximization requires that long run marginal cost be equated to selling price and that long-run marginal cost be increasing.

Further attention to the appropriate role of financial assets, in explanation of firms' behavior, is addressed in the final chapter of this study.

Macroeconomics

Macroeconomic analysis has focussed on the role of investment in inventories and inventory adjustments, in relation to the business cycle (or level of business activity). We can characterize this type of study as composed of three branches:

1. Theoretical—Metzler, Lovell, and others.

2. Statistical studies, sponsored in many cases by the National Bureau of Research, or Office of Business Economics of the Department of Commerce. Works in this category include those by Abramovitz, Mack, and Stanback.

3. Econometric studies,[25] with an ultimate goal of providing predictive models for the economy. Work in this category includes that of Darling, Evans, Klein, and Pashigian.

Since any one paper can fit into more than one of the categories above, there is a good deal of overlapping in the coverage, and these divisions, in consequence, are suggestive, rather than definitive.

The classic theoretical article is Metzler's,[26] and it has provided a basis for much of the subsequent research in this field. He supposes that firms attempt to maintain a constant ratio of inventory to sales. A Lundberg model is used, in which consumer demand responds immediately to change in income, while changes in output of consumer goods lag one period behind changes in sales. An expectations coefficient is also introduced.

In its most general form, the model derived is:

$$y_t = [(1+n)(1+a) + 1] \cdot B \cdot y_{t-1} - (1+2n)(1+a)B \cdot y_{t-2}$$
$$+ (1-a)n \cdot B \cdot y_{t-3} + v_0, \tag{2.5}$$

where y_t = total income of the economy for period t, v_0 = net investment (which in Metzler's numerical examples was always held constant for each succeeding period, after a change from the value for the first period (the purpose of the latter change—to provide an initial jolt to the economy), B = marginal propensity to consume—$0 < B < 1$, n = coefficient of expectations, which equals the ratio of the change in sales expected for this period, divided by the observed change in sales over the period preceding, $-1 < n < 1$, and a = inventory accelerator, i.e., the ratio of inventory divided by sales which manufacturers will hold. In his numerical examples, Metzler used values of $0 < a < 1$, but suggested values > 1 as possible.

It is evident that equation (2.5) is in the form of a third order difference equation (or second order, for values of $n = 0$). Depending on values chosen for the three parameters, and the roots found for the equation, the path of (y) over time can show cyclical or unstable behavior.

Metzler's model is elegant in its simplicity, and the cyclical behavior it is capable of demonstrating is strongly suggestive of an inventory/business cycle link, thereby fulfilling the intent of the work. However, as pointed out by Metzler himself, for any positive value of the coefficient of expectations, rather severe restrictions exist for the stability of the system. For such a case, stable solutions require either unrealistically low values assigned to the MPC, and/or very low (e.g., $n < 0.1$) accelerator values.

There are any number of questions which might be posed of the Metzler model. Some of these would be:

1. Inventory is a stock value, while sales over a period represent a flow. Hence the numerical value of the accelerator is directly affected by the length[27] of period chosen. What is the proper length?

2. Is the assumption that a constant inventory/sales ratio is desired by firms consistent with profit-maximizing behavior? Following Whitin,[28] it would be more realistic, perhaps, to have inventory holdings desired which were proportional to the square root of sales.

3. The Keynesian approach suggests that unanticipated drawdown of inventory serves as a firm's signal to increase production.[29] This implies that proper production level is the key decision facing the firm, rather than maintenance of a "proper" inventory level. The two are necessarily related, of course—the question is, which is the tail and which is the dog?

More broadly, however, it is reasonable to conclude that fashioning a dynamic concept to illustrate cyclical behavior represents a valuable contribution by Metzler, and that the weaknesses of the model reflect simplistic assumptions about manufacturers' behavior—intended to illustrate the mechanics of the model, rather than to definitively describe real behavior.

A series of studies have followed, designed to improve on the foundation provided by Metzler. Klein and Popkin[30] used a flexible accelerator, which provided for *partial* adjustment of inventory level in one period. Darling[31] provided the variable accelerator, which allowed for variation in the inventory/sales ratio as well as in the speed of adjustment. And, in the spirit of the Keynesian buffer stock approach, Lovell[32] introduced a coefficient of anticipations (for manufacturers' expectations of anticipated changes in sales), which was used in conjunction with a flexible accelerator.

The main thrust of the latter studies was toward relations which would provide for better prediction of the effects of changes in inventory investment upon the economy. And for this reason, both Lovell[33] and Darling[34] also utilized unfilled orders as an additional variable in their models, based on its contribution as an explanatory variable, more than for specific theoretical reason. In general, the lag structures which have evolved with these various approaches (as well as other parallel efforts not cited) reflect "best empirical evidence," rather than theoretical interpretation of manufacturers' behavior.

Realizing the importance of anticipations, Pashigian[35] and Hirsch and Lovell[36] experimented with the then experimental Department of Commerce series of manufacturers' anticipated forthcoming quarterly sales. This series is issued annually in the first quarter of the year, and not surprisingly, manufacturers' anticipations for first quarter sales corresponded fairly closely to actual first quarter sales—and, rather less well for succeeding quarters. These attempts can be considered unsuccessful.

In the meantime, major statistical studies to characterize the inventory behavior of U.S. industry were undertaken by a number of researchers. Some of the most important, sponsored by the NBER, were those of Stanback,[37] Mack,[38] and Abramovits.[39] In keeping with the long-term study objectives of the NBER, these works focussed on the interplay between inventories and the business cycle. Broadly, these studies showed more or less constant ratios of manufacturers' inventories to sales—but with the emphasis on *more or less,* rather than on constant. In fact, as a cyclical function, inventory accumulation (decumulation) lags sales increases (decreases), thereby making inventory change a lagging cyclical indicator.

One observation of particular significance relates to the *size* of the fluctuation in inventory investment. As Stanback[40] reported,

> Inventory changes have contributed very significantly to cyclical fluctuation, accounting for 70 percent of all declines in gross national product during post-war recessions and about 25 percent of all increases in GNP during the first year of each postwar expansion.

Or, as reported from another source,[41] "... if 75 percent of the fluctuation in inventory adjustment could be controlled, the economy would not have had any postwar business recessions."

The Joint Economic Committee[42] of the 87th Congress responded with vigorous interest to such pronouncements. Hearings were held, in 1962, on "Inventory Fluctuations and Economic Stabilization." The expressed objective of the hearings was investigation of "the role inventory changes may play in magnifying economic recessions and booms," and to weigh the possibilities of smoothing out inventory fluctuations by some type of governmental action (e.g., perhaps tax concessions for holders of excess inventories).

To the hearings were invited an array of economic talent—including many whose works are cited in this section. However, after lengthy testimony and deliberation, the consensus was reached that, while changes in inventory adjustment were large in proportion to cyclical swings in GNP, inventory changes were best considered symptomatic of the cyclical behavior, rather than causative of it. As a result, there were no legislative consequences to the hearings, but attendant interest bestowed upon the subject may well have helped stimulate additional research.

An additional, noteworthy contribution of the period and also presented at the JEC hearings[43] was made by Holt et al.,[44] with their concept of linear decision rules for manufacturers, based on micro-model cost-minimizing production decisions.

This approach was, in turn, later utilized in the valuable research of Belsley.[45] He approached the problem of the manufacturer's production (inventory investment) problem from a different direction than the econometric studies cited above:

1. First, a complete differentiation was made for the decision process appropriate to processes producing to order (which hold essentially no inventories of finished goods, but do accumulate unfilled orders), and those producing to stock (for which the reverse is true). Observation that this differentiation existed was not novel, but its incorporation into a cohesive and detailed analysis is notable.[46]

2. By relating manufacturers' decisions to the linear production rules mentioned above, Belsley was able to demonstrate how unfilled orders and stocks of finished goods enter into the production decision within the framework of profit-maximizing behavior.

In the development of the next three chapters of this paper, Belsley's example will be used and expanded upon.

Industrial Management and Operations Research

The thrust from this branch of analysis has been directed at optimal management of inventory and planning of production from a cost-minimizing (or profit contribution maximizing) standpoint. In fact, as one author remarks, "The appearance of advanced studies of inventory coincided with the birth of operations research."[47]

As earlier noted,[48] Eli Clemens and others have shown that much industrial output comes from multi-product plants, with production in blocks or lots of manufacture. One of the basic production planning problems, then, is the economic lot scheduling problem (ELSP).

The ELSP problem has several dimensions. First, for individual products produced (one at a time) on a single production line, an economic manufacturing quantity can be calculated, based on product demand, production setup cost, costs of maintaining inventory, and the like. This suggests a normally cyclical, or rotating, pattern of production. However, the situation may arise that production time is required for two or more products at once, but since only one product can be made at a time, there is "interference." The question then posed is how to proceed with the resulting schedule on a cost-minimizing (or profit-maximizing) basis? Or, better stated, recognizing that interference may arise, how best should the schedule be organized to begin with?

As Elmaghraby[49] makes clear, the ELSP is more than a single problem with a singular solution. It is really a branch of study which has been analyzed under a variety of conditions, including:

1. Uncertainty of requirements (i.e., demand) for products.[50]

2. Multi-stage production cycles[51] through which the product must pass.

3. Variable costs for changes in production pattern, or of ordering for components and raw materials.

4. The impact of cash flow considerations.

Answers, or more properly, the approach toward answering this family of problems on a dynamic programming basis, can be broadly put into two categories. First, there are the analytical approaches "that achieve the optimum of a restricted version of the original problem."[52] And second, "heuristic approaches[53] that achieve 'good,' and sometimes 'very good,' solutions of the original problem."

The first approach has in it some of the logical elements of the standard microeconomic approach—i.e., simplification of the problem to enable specific mathematical treatment. However, it differs in that any particular solution is based (more or less closely) upon the data of a specific production line. It is, of course, in the second category, that the operations research approach is most clearly differentiated from standard economic analysis. Here, the objective is a "workable" answer for a complex (real) situation—i.e., a "nuts and bolts," rather than a theoretical, answer.

We might also interpret the ELSP as suggesting that a key factor, in the decision on product run length, is provision of sufficient finished product to enable normal schedule rotation before again finding it necessary to produce the same product. The resulting inventory would be viewed as one held against projected demand for the product—quite a different motive than the holding of inventory for buffer purposes (i.e., for unexpected changes in demand). This point will be explored further, later in this paper.

While the review above of ELSP provides something of the flavor of the approaches used, and problems dealt with, there are many other directions of interest and effort in the overall field of inventory management and production planning.

In parts and raw materials inventory management, a revolution of sorts has occurred with the adoption of computer based systems to replace the "rules of thumb" in prevalent use just twenty years ago.[54] The *system* needs, and hence the approach taken, range from simple replenishment situations in which the inventoried items are ordered from outside suppliers (the case with retailers), to the other extreme, of firms using the finished product of one process as the raw material for another (e.g., chemical companies).

In the machinery and fabricated metals industries, it is common to have very large numbers of fasteners, components, and other small parts which may have widespread but scattered usage in a variety of products within one firm. To control the inventory and reorder of such items, systems of material requirements planning (MRP),[55] are coming into widespread use. Broadly, these are of two types: (1) pull—or replenishment requesting by using point, and (2) push—or replenishment arising from production record analysis by the supplying point within the firm.

In either case, computer systems are used to correlate usage of each component from the standpoint of its required aliquot in every production run. This information enables constant updating and tracking of the inventory status of (a very large number of) components vs. scheduled production, and consequent reorder needs. By keeping track of inventory, rate of usage, and reorder needs, many companies have been able to significantly reduce inventory investment. The concept does not differ materially from what has always been done "by hand" for a few major components or raw materials which made up 40 percent, perhaps, of raw material inventory. The difference lies in an economically efficient system which can be extended to the other 60 percent.

Whether in the production planning, or the inventory management area, a key input in operations research analyses are cost data. The normal source of cost information would be the local plant's accounting system. However, the conventions used in allocation or separation of fixed and semi-variable costs tend to vary substantially between locations, and often embody relatively simplistic assumptions. Practitioners (of operations research) are discovering that substantial dividends are paid by carefully surveying cost data, and using concepts and procedures, appropriate to the purpose of a particular planning model, in specifying costs.[56]

The inclusion of appropriate opportunity costs may well be required. For instance, there is the implication that if savings are made in inventory investment, lower inventory holdings are needed. However, a trade-off exists[57] between the ability of the firm to reliably supply its customers vs. levels of inventory held. The solution could be simply the specification of a (high) target level for service reliability. However, target levels, per se, may offer no more than simple subjective estimates. The real answer lies in the development of criteria, based on likely customer reaction, to the effects on demand facing the firm (and profit effect) vs. different levels of less-than-perfect service.

The above coverage of the operations research area is representative in nature, and provides a flavor of the approaches used. For detail and thorough coverage of the status of inventory management and production planning systems, an excellent starting point is the survey article by Harvey M. Wagner referenced in the notes.

3

Development of a Profit-Maximizing Model

In the preceding chapter, obstacles in the path of a firm attempting to use the micro profit-maximizing rule[1] were reviewed. This chapter explores an approach from a different direction, developed by Holt, Modigliani, Muth, and Simon.[2,3]

Their analysis considers a decision-maker attempting to maximize costs, which are represented by U-shaped average cost curves. While derivation of the specific relations expressing these costs may not be possible, it is relatively simple to develop quadratic expressions which approximate the underlying function. The particularly attractive feature of this strategy is that differentiation of the quadratic expression(s), as a step toward the minimization, yields, as the final result, linear equations (or "decision rules").

The technique is a versatile one, which can be applied in a variety of circumstances. The example below demonstrates its use in a particular case.

Suppose one were to collect all costs of an operation, manufacturing a single homogeneous good, and distribute them over the following three categories:

1. All the costs (i.e., both variable and fixed) of producing at a given level (C_p).

2. All the costs incurred in changing from one level of production to another (C_{DP}). (These will include the costs involved in changing the rate of output from existing facilities, but not including investment costs to *change* facilities.)

3. All the costs involved (C_H), in holding an inventory of finished goods (including the opportunity cost of lost sales because of insufficient stocks).

It is assumed that these cost categories are represented by U-shaped average cost curves, which can therefore be approximated by appropriate quadratic equations. On this basis, for period (t), we would have:

$$C_P = a_o + a_1 \cdot P_t + a_2 \cdot P_t^2 \tag{3.1}$$

$$C_{DP} = b_o + b_1 \cdot DP + b_2 \cdot DP^2 \tag{3.2}$$

$$C_H = c_o + c_1 \cdot H_t + c_2 \cdot H_t^2 \tag{3.3}$$

where P_t = production for this period, and P_{t-1}, the period preceding, H_t = inventory held at the end of this period, and H_{t-1} at the end of the preceding period, μ_t = sales expectations for this period, $DP = P_t - P_{t-1}$, and

$$P_t = \mu_t + H_t - H_{t-1}, \text{ or,}$$

$$H_t = P_t - \mu_t + H_{t-1}. \tag{3.4}$$

(Values of coefficients a, b, and c are discussed below.)

Total cost for period (t), C_t, will be the sum of the individual costs: C_P, C_{DP}, and C_H. Summing the three expressions, but ignoring the constant terms, which will disappear in the differentiation step below, yields:

$$C_t = a_1 \cdot P_t + a_2 \cdot P_t^2 + b_1 \cdot DP + b_2 \cdot DP^2$$
$$+ c_1 \cdot H_t + c_2 \cdot H_t^2 \tag{3.5}$$

Next, we substitute $(P_t - P_{t-1})$ for DP, and $(P_t - \mu_t + H_{t-1})$ for H_t. Then, differentiating C_t with respect to P_t produces:

$$\frac{dC}{DP} = (a_1 + b_1 + c_1) - 2b_2 P_{t-1} + 2c_2 H_{t-1}$$

$$- 2c_2 \mu_t + 2(a_2 + b_2)P_t + 2c_2 P_t \tag{3.6}$$

To determine the profit-maximizing (cost-minimizing) level of production, we set $DC/dP = 0$, and solve for P_t.

$$P_t = \frac{-(a_1 + b_1 + c_1)}{2(a_2 + b_2 + c_2)} + \frac{b_2}{a_2 + b_2 + c_2} \times P_{t-1}$$

$$- \frac{c_2}{a_2 + b_2 + c_2} \cdot H_{t-1} + \frac{c_2}{a_2 + b_2 + c_2} \cdot \mu_t \cdot \tag{3.7}$$

Now, while we do not necessarily know the coefficients of the original equations (nor of 3.5), we do have something of particular interest in equation (3.7). It relates a profit-maximizing level of production for the present period to sales expectations, and the previous period's level of finished goods inventory and production. Indeed, intuitively, it would seem entirely reasonable to expect the profit-maximizing firm to consider precisely these variables in establishing the level of production for the forthcoming period (unless, of course, the firm's production process were the sort which accumulated unfilled orders, in which case these should be considered, as well).

Not knowing the values of the coefficients means, of course, that we cannot use equation (3.7) as a decision rule. However, we can certainly use the expression as a means of testing the firm's behavior, to see if, in fact, its production decisions have been consistent with profit-maximizing behavior. For the latter purpose, we may just as well simplify the coefficients of (3.7) to yield:

$$P_t = d_0 + d_1 \cdot P_{t-1} + d_2 \cdot H_{t-1} + d_3 \cdot \mu_t \cdot \qquad (3.8)$$

And, of course, this expression is very similar to equation (2.1), in spite of its completely different derivation.[4] In fact, were we to regression test equation (3.8), unless there were a reliable set of "ex ante" sales expectations available for the purpose, the best proxy to use would probably be the sales actually realized for each period—and, in this form the two relations are identical.

Before testing, however, we should consider what restrictions have been imposed on us by the "single homogeneous good" assumption. Is the model valid *only* for single good firms (and are there any)?—or, for the multi-product firm, must the rule be separately applied for each product?

These questions are rhetorical, of course, but they serve to illustrate an important point about decision rule models, and their uses. A manager's decision on appropriate production level for the next period does not consist simply of obtaining a value for each of the factors H_{t-1}, P_{t-1}, and μ_t and then, with the proper set of coefficients, using a calculator to solve for P_t. Indeed, that would be putting the cart before the horse.

Instead, the manager's task is to sift through a large amount of data (neither necessarily complete, nor accurate at the time a decision is needed). The data are subdivided into many segments of which costs and other financial information, and items relating to customer requirements are the most important.[5] Based on this, the manager makes a profit-maximizing decision (as we, and he, would like to think). If indeed the production decision is one more in a series of correct choices, our use of the "decision rule" will confirm it—assuming, of course, a correctly derived expression.

Use of the decision rule to see if the producer is acting *as if* he were making profit-maximizing decisions removes the largest objection to testing such a model in the multi-product firm case. The separate pieces of information on inventory, or previous production rate of each product are not needed for individual decision purposes, and we can conveniently use the overall results to judge how closely they conform to our model.

In similar vein, would it be permissible to aggregate a group of firms, such as we might find in any given industry? It is true that the further the process of aggregation is carried, the greater the number of potential problems (e.g., compensating errors, differentials in cost structures and rates of response, et al.). On the other hand, such a step would make available for test purposes the excellent series of data on "Manufacturers' Shipments, Inventories, and Orders," which is compiled by the U.S. Department of Commerce, Bureau of the Census.

The M-3 data series for the 1958-1976 period are available for individual two-digit Census industries, either seasonally adjusted or unadjusted, and with both monthly and quarterly data. Since it is the intention in this study to use this source of data, if found feasible, and bearing in mind the caveats above, it would seem a reasonable step to perform the tests suggested above on some representative industries to see what the results might be.

There is another factor to be considered. Equation (3.8) is based upon sales expectations. The M-3 data series provides actual new order/sales statistics, but *not* expectations. With the premise that firms use their sales organizations not only to secure orders, but to provide reasonable projections of forward sales expectations, we shall be, in other words, simultaneously testing not only conformance to a decision rule, but also for accuracy of sales expectations vs. realized sales. Fortunately, some of the results obtained later support the reasonability of this assumption. We shall use new orders received, N_t, as a proxy for μ_t in the initial testing of the equation (3.8) model.

The final characteristic to be noted of the M-3 series is that there are no production data. Production statistics may be derived from the data presented, as will be further developed in this study. For our immediate purposes, the relation expressed by equation (3.4) will be used—an assumption later to be modified.

Industries to be Studied

The Bureau of Census has divided manufacturing activities into nineteen two-digit categories, nine of which produce nondurable goods and ten, durable goods. The present study examines nine of these, listed below, as a representative selection.

Type of Goods	Census Industry Number	Name of Industry
Nondurable	20	Food Products
Nondurable	21	Tobacco Manufactures

Nondurable	26	Paper and Allied Products
Nondurable	27	Printing and Publishing
Nondurable	28	Chemical and Allied Products
Nondurable	29	Petroleum and Coal Products
Durable	34	Fabricated Metal Products
Durable	35	Machinery, except Electrical
Durable	36	Electrical Machinery

Why a "representative selection" should include six of the nine nondurable goods industries, and only three of the durable goods is a topic decided later in this chapter.

The test model for an OLSQ regression is derived directly from equation (3.8), with substitution of new orders received, N_t, as proxy for sales expectations of the period, and with addition of an error term, e_t.

$$P_t = d_0 + d_1 \cdot P_{t-1} + d_2 \cdot H_{t-1} + d_3 \cdot N_t + e_t. \tag{3.9}$$

Results of the test, using quarterly Census data (nonseasonally adjusted) are presented in table 1. Standard errors for the coefficients are tabulated under them (in parentheses). Coefficients significant at the 5 percent level, by the standard two-tailed test, are marked with asterisks. In addition to R^2's for each regression, the table indicates whether, or not, unfilled orders are reported in the Census data for that particular industry.

What are expectations for coefficients d_1, d_2, and d_3?

1. Since d_1 reflects consideration of the costs involved in changes of production level, it would be expected that $d_1 > 0$, and larger, the more this type of cost consideration weighs.

2. Based on the buffer-stock motive for holding finished goods inventories, the larger H_{t-1} is, the smaller need production be for the forthcoming period, so we expect $d_2 < 0$.

3. To the extent that increased sales will call for increased production, we expect $d_3 > 0$.

As table 1 shows, all the d_3 coefficients appear significant, and most of the d_1 and d_2 coefficients as well. The R^2 results indicate good fits of the data to the decision rule. Most of the coefficients appear to have proper signs, and in most cases sales anticipations seem to be the dominant factor in the production decision.

One specific relation, which does not fulfill expectations is the comparison of the d_2's and d_3's. From equation (3.7), we would expect these coefficients to be equal in magnitude, but of opposite sign. For the first six industries, the signs are correctly opposed, but not for the latter three. In

Table 1. Regression Results for Nine Industries: an Initial Test

Ind. No.	Industry	d_0	d_1	d_2	d_3	$\underline{R}^2$	Unfilled Orders
20	Food Prod.	315*	.0019	-0.511*	1.087*	.9994	No
		(103)	(.0433)	(.102)	(.034)		
21	Tobacco Prod.	-67*	.0756	-0.211*	1.003*	.9906	No
		(26)	(.0565)	(.077)	(.056)		
26	Paper	84	.393*	-0.672	.695*	.9933	Yes
		(68)	(.110)	(.359)	(.091)		
27	Printing	1.33	.0974*	-0.245*	.934*	.9993	Yes
		(20)	(.0206)	(.109)	(.022)		
28	Chemical	38	.0670*	-0.156*	.971*	.9995	No
		(45)	(.0225)	(.056)	(.021)		
29	Petroleum	395*	.0196	-0.543*	1.020*	.9998	No
		(78)	(.0257)	(.105)	(.021)		
34	Fab. Metals	125	.302*	.684*	.558*	.9931	Yes
		(128)	(.072)	(.148)	(.053)		
35	Machinery	-347	.549*	.688*	.308*	.9869	Yes
		(218)	(.095)	(.272)	(.051)		
36	Electrical	29	.534*	.130	.442*	.9869	Yes
		(159)	(.098)	(.328)	(.072)		

NOTE: $P_t = d_0 + d_1 P_{t-1} + d_2 H_{t-1} + d_3 N_t + e_t$.

[a] Standard errors in parenthesis, under coefficients.

[b] Coefficients, significant at the 5 percent level, are marked by *.

addition, only in the case of Industry 26 are the magnitudes of d_2 and d_3 reasonably matched. The obvious question, of course, is, "What's wrong?" The answer, in good part, lies in the fact that H is a stock quantity, defined in value at the end of a period. N is a flow quantity whose size is directly related to the length of the data period chosen. Quite obviously, equality of magnitude of d_2 and d_3 is a function of the length of data period chosen, in addition to the underlying relation indicated. From inspection of the results of the test, we could tentatively conclude that for the first six industries, a period shorter than a quarter would have produced results more consistent with this particular expectation.

There are some other intriguing observations to make:

1. The d_3 coefficients for the three durable goods industries have positive signs as expected (and indeed, explanation of a negative d_3 sign would be difficult)! However, the coefficients themselves are in the .3 to .6 range, or roughly only half the size of the d_3's for the nondurable goods industries.

2. Two other durable/nondurable differences stand out. While the size of the d_2 coefficients for the durable industries is in the same general size range as the nondurables', the sign is different. Also, the size of the d_1 coefficients would suggest that the level of production in the period just past is as important a factor in deciding durable goods output for the new period as are sales expectations.

   Taken together, these observations would suggest, as a simple explanation, that the production function for the durable goods industries differs from nondurables. However, there is more than that to the story.

3. If we look again at the table, we see that the size of the d_1 and d_3 coefficients for the paper industry, 26, are rather close to those of Industries 34, 35, and 36, and rather different than those of the other five nondurable goods industries.

   And the nondurable industry with the next largest d_1 and next smallest d_3 is Industry 27.

4. The final observation relates to the very right hand column of our list of industries, which shows which of the nine under examination accumulate unfilled orders, which are reported by the Bureau of Census. All three durable goods industries, plus Industries 26 and 27, accumulate unfilled orders.

In other words, the point has been raised that the inter-industry differences observed may relate more to the parameter represented by unfilled orders[6], than to the durable/nondurable distinction.

Unfilled orders, in fact, are accumulated by all ten durable goods industry of the BuCensus 2-digit category, and by three of the nine nondurable goods industries as well. The nine industries selected for this study include four nondurable industries which do not accumulate unfilled orders (Industries 20, 21, 28, 29), and two which do (Industries 26, 27). These plus three durable goods industries (Industries 34, 35, 36) which also accumulate unfilled orders, were chosen to represent a cross-section of industrial behaviour.

How industries with unfilled orders differ from those without is the subject of the next chapter.

4

Production to Order and Production to Stock

Customers are able to buy fresh bread from the local baker's stock. Bread is a relatively homogeneous product and the baker needs to stock only a modest number of varieties. If demand exceeds the available stock of any one sort of loaf, the baker incurs the opportunity cost of lost sales.

Wedding cakes, on the other hand, are a more heterogeneous sort of product. What one customer wants would not exactly suit another, so they are ordered in advance by customers and prepared to individual specification by the baker. Orders that have been received for cakes not yet delivered are "unfilled orders." The accumulation of unfilled orders noted in chapter 3 relates to the production by some industries of goods to order.

Observations of the differences between *production to stock* and *production to order* have been made for some time. The distinction appears in Abramovitz's[1] studies. Ruth Mack[2] emphasized the role of unfilled orders as viewed by the customer—i.e., that materials on order but not yet delivered were additive to those already on hand (in inventory) in defining "materials in sight" for planning purposes. Victor Zarnowitz[3] reported durable goods industries as producing principally to order, and both he and Stanback[4] measured the changes in size of backlogs of unfilled orders over the course of business cycles. Darling,[5] Lovell,[6] and Klein,[7] among others, incorporated unfilled orders into estimated equations for flexible accelerator type models portraying manufacturers' inventory investment.

In the latter studies, unfilled orders were found useful as explanatory variables which improved the fit of empirical test results, but little was presented as rationale to make clear how unfilled orders were related to other factors underlying production decisions. In fact, the focus of these studies on *inventory investment* as a macro-variable[8] probably has tended to divert attention from the (directly) related production decision process.

However, as our metaphorical baker has illustrated above, the processes of production to order and production to stock have quite different characteristics, even though both may be conducted simultaneously by the same small firm. Lack of a clear differentiation between the two processes has encouraged, as a rather persistent error in the literature, the treatment of finished goods inventory *less unfilled orders* as equal to a *net* finished goods inventory. (We doubt that our baker would compute *his* net finished goods inventory by subtracting unfilled orders for wedding cakes from his stock of bread.)

The needed clarification was provided in 1969 in a valuable contribution by David Belsley.[9] His approach was to establish a cost-minimizing micro-theoretical basis for production decisions for both order and stock production processes. Then he tested the observed (two-digit) industries' behavior against the derived model with considerable success. Belsley's lead is closely followed in the development of this chapter.

Production *to* stock implies, of course, that sales are *from* stock, as figure 3 shows. Unless $P^s = S^s$, there will be a difference between the rates of sales and production during a period, and hence a change in the stock of finished goods.

$$P_t^s - S_t^s = \Delta H_t \tag{4.1}$$

where P_t^s = production to stock, during period (t), S_t^s = sales from inventory, during period (t), ΔH_t = change in H over period (t) $\equiv H_t - H_{t-1}$.

Figure 3.   The Stock/Order Distinction

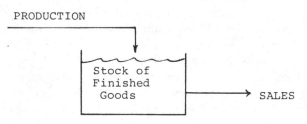

Production to Stock

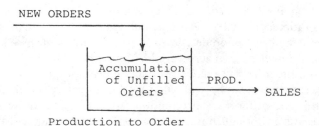

Production to Order

Production to order on the other hand means simply that production is undertaken only after an order is received. To the extent that the customer takes possession of the goods promptly upon completion, $P^o = S^o$. During any given period, new orders, N^o, are received which increase the accumulation of unfilled orders, U. At the same time, as goods are finished and deliveries/sales are made, U is diminished.

$$P^o_t = S^o_t = N^o_t - \Delta U_t \tag{4.2}$$

where P^o_t = production to order, during period (t), S^o_t = sales of production to order during (t), N^o_t = new orders (for goods to order) during (t), U_t = unfilled orders at the end of (t), and ΔU_t = change in U over period (t) $\equiv U_t - U_{t-1}$.

In the relations above, the (s) and (o) superscripts were not used for H and U. The omission is more than a desirable simplification—it is a reasonable approximation of the actual case for the following reasons:

1. Producers of the relatively homogeneous types of goods typically made to stock might well *want* to accumulate U. However, if one producer were out of stock of a given product at some point in time, the customer need not wait, because the good would normally be immediately available from an alternate supplier. In other words, competition effectively limits the accumulation of unfilled orders by producers to stock.[10]

   Additional support for this premise is that the Department of Commerce does not collect and publish U for industries producing only to stock. And, in turn, not having an accumulation of unfilled orders means that new orders may be considered to convert directly to sales:

$$N^s_t \equiv S^s_t \tag{4.3}$$

2. As to the accumulation of inventories of finished goods, of the types normally made to order, there are a number of possibilities.[11] The most important are: (a) goods held for sample or demonstration purpose, (b) delays between completion of production and shipment/delivery to customer, and (c) order cancellations (with or without penalty).

   Here the argument would be that such goods do not represent a stock which, in general, can be used for immediate filling of new orders. In addition, the amount of goods in this category is probably such a minor proportion of overall sales and production that H is not a matter of practical importance. Hence, we are saying that completion of production to order is followed promptly by sale, or:

$$P^o_t \equiv S^o_t \tag{4.4}$$

The Profit-Maximizing Level of Production

In the previous chapter, Holt and Modigliani's approach, of a quadratic cost function approximating an actual U-shaped cost curve, was used to derive equation (3.8). It is now apparent, within the terminology of this chapter, that it was actually the cost-minimizing level of a *production to stock* process which was developed. And, rewriting (3.8) with the appropriate superscripts gives us:

$$P_t^s = b_0 + b_1 \cdot P_{t-1}^s + b_2 \cdot H_{t-1} + b_3 \cdot \mu_t^s, \qquad (4.5)$$

where μ_t^s = expectations of sales from stock for the period.

In precisely parallel fashion, the cost-minimizing level of a *production to order* process, p_t^o, can be derived. In this case, the quadratic expression for the costs of holding inventory will be replaced by one expressing the costs of holding unfilled orders, U.

While the mathematical steps are the same, the concepts relating to the costs of holding unfilled orders are less intuitively evident than those associated with holding inventory—for, after all, inventory is "real" and requires workers to move it, warehouses to store it, and insurance protection.

Belsley suggests that for unfilled orders, the most important factors are:

1. The risk, or opportunity costs, of cancellations and of lost sales, which increase as customer waiting times are longer—i.e., as U is larger.

2. Offsetting this, at least in part, are the potential economies the firm will encounter, as waiting periods are longer, for opportunities to group orders for more efficient production.

A factor of significance, but not identified by Belsley, would be:

3. The contribution to maximizing the present value of the firm by converting unfilled orders to sales sooner, rather than later—and, hence, there is a penalty to present value in the form of an opportunity cost, the larger U is allowed to become.

With these factors in mind, the derivation of the profit-maximizing level, for a production to order process, produces:

$$P_t^o = a_0 + a_1 P_{t-1}^o + a_2 \cdot U_{t-1} + a_3 \cdot \mu_t^o. \qquad (4.6)$$

Production to either Order or Stock

Equations (4.5) and (4.6) were derived as linear decision rules for firms producing only to stock, or only to order, respectively. However, the intention was earlier expressed of testing equations of this sort against Department of Commerce time series data for two-digit *industries*. We must address the question of whether entire industries conform to one pattern or the other. The answer is "yes" and "no."

The absence of an accumulation of unfilled orders for six of the nine nondurable goods industries, as noted in chapter 4, can be taken as evidence of little enough production to order activity to warrant treatment as if they produced only to stock. (Four of these six are included in the present study.)

However, while there are individual firms which produce only to order,[12] there are no industries which do so. The remainder of the nondurable goods industries, and all durable goods industries, report *both* finished goods inventories, and unfilled orders. In other words, like the baker at the beginning of this chapter, there is production to *both* stock and order. This does not rule out the use of equation (4.5) and (4.6) for empirical testing per se—but it would require that the sales data for each industry then be available in subdivided form, separately reporting sales from stock and sales to order. This, however, is not the case, and a different approach is needed.

Production to both Order and Stock[13]

When a firm produces to both order and stock, we might well wonder whether (or to what degree) the decisions on optimal P_t^s and P_t^o are independent. In the case of our invaluable baker, would the two decisions be uninfluenced by each other? Or is it likely that constraints on the availability of any factor(s) of production (e.g., available oven space, shelf space, personnel, etc.) might require judicious choice between allocation toward making more bread at the expense of cake (or vice versa)? Similarly, the possession of a "comfortable" inventory of bread might at one time permit taking on additional orders for cakes, while a "tight" bread inventory might suggest a lower current cake output.

Taking this as a lead, it would seem logical to express the cost-minimizing levels for P_t^s and P_t^o as structural models, each of which contain terms relating to the decision factors for both types of production. In other words, the expressions should contain both "own" and "cross" factors, as below:

$$P_t^o = c_0 + c_1 P_{t-1}^s + c_2 P_{t-1}^o + c_3 H_{t-1}$$
$$+ c_4 U_{t-1} + c_5 \mu_t^s + c_6 \mu_t^o + w \qquad (4.7)$$

$$P_t^s = d_0 + d_1 P_{t-1}^s + d_2 P_{t-1}^o + d_3 H_{t-1}$$
$$+ d_4 U_{t-1} + d_5 \mu_t^s + d_6 \mu_t^o + w'. \qquad (4.8)$$

In the latter equation, the coefficients d_1, d_3, and d_5 compare directly with those of (4.5) for the "own" factors; and d_2, d_4, and d_6 represent the effects on the elements which relate to production to order (the cross effects) from (4.6). (The w's represent error terms.)

We must remember, of course, that the firm's total production will be the sum of production to order and to stock:

$$P_t^o + P_t^s \equiv P_t \tag{4.9}$$

And similarly for sales expectations, and actual sales:

$$\mu_t^o + \mu_t^s \equiv \mu_t \tag{4.10}$$

$$S_t^o + S_t^s \equiv S_t \tag{4.11}$$

Since (4.7) and (4.8) are additive per (4.9), and because of the similarity of their form, we can express total production (cost minimizing) as:

$$P_t = n_0 + n_1 P_{t-1}^s + n_2 P_{t-1}^o + n_3 H_{t-1}$$
$$+ n_4 U_{t-1} + n_5 \mu_t^s + n_6 \mu_t^o + w'' \tag{4.12}$$

And, we note that the coefficients of (4.12) are individually summed from those of (4.7) and (4.8).

$$c_i + d_i = n_i. \tag{4.13}$$

Equation (4.13), together with its immediate precedents, (4.7) and (4.8), have two valuable features: (1) They have been derived as production decision rules within a profit-maximizing (cost-minimizing) context; (2) they enable (given availability of appropriate data) simultaneous but individual estimation of the two different production processes.

There is, however, a major problem to be overcome—four of the six explanatory variables appearing in the set of equations are not available data: P_{t-1}^o, P_{t-1}^s, μ_t^o, and μ_t^s. For the first two there is the additional, but not really serious, impediment that the Department of Commerce's Manufacturers time series does not include production statistics. This poses no real problem. By utilizing (4.4) and (4.1), overall production can easily be deduced from reported sales and inventory figures.

$$P_t^o = S_t^o, \text{ and, by addition,} \tag{4.4}$$

$$\frac{P_t^s = S_t^s + \Delta H_t}{P_t = S_t + \Delta H_t} \tag{4.1}$$
$$\tag{4.14}$$

What *is* a problem is that there is no differentiation in the data for sales to order vs. sales from inventory (as noted earlier); nor would the collection of such data seem feasible in the future. To round out the lot, neither are sales expectations statistics feasible (whether μ_t^s, μ_t^o, or overall expectations, μ_t). Experimental series on manufacturers' expectations have been evaluated from time to time, with mediocre to poor results for explanatory forecasting purposes.[14,15,16] (Expectations are not "hard" data.)

What *is* a part of the Census data are statistics on actual sales realized and new orders received, and one would hope that this information could be used appropriately as a proxy for expectations. How this can be done is covered in the next section.

Derivation of a Testable Model

Before equations (4.7), (4.8), and (4.12) can be empirically tested, some means must be found of introducing factors for which data are available for the explanatory variables: P_{t-1}^o, P_{t-1}^s, μ_t^s, and μ_t^o; and for the dependent variables: P_t^o and P_t^s.

Following Belsley's lead, five steps are needed

1. The first assumption is that sales expectations, for sales from inventory, are unbiased, i.e.:

$$N_t^s \equiv S_t^s = \mu_t^s + \epsilon_t \tag{4.15}$$

or simply, that any forecasting error is independent of sales.

Results which we shall inspect later in this study lend credibility to this approximation. Why then have published efforts to collect and use the experimental statistical series for manufacturer's sales expectations been unrewarding?

The answer seems to be that the expectations of producers to stock are relatively precise in the short term, and progressively further from the mark as the forecasting period lengthens. In other words, if a manufacturer is asked in February what his quarterly sales expectations are for the whole year, his first quarter's estimate is excellent; after all, February is the current month, March only a month away, and January is already in the bag. The accuracy of forecast for succeeding quarters is lower. But, since our models are based on sales estimates made at the beginning of each period, approximation of μ_t^s by N_t^s poses no problem.

2. Next we can eliminate the P_{t-1}^o and μ_t^o terms. By utilizing (4.9) and (4.10), we have:

$$P^o_{t-1} = P_{t-1} + P^s_{t-1}, \text{ and,} \tag{4.16}$$

$$\mu^o_t = \mu_t + \mu^s_t; \tag{4.17}$$

and the right-hand side expressions will be substituted in each case for the left-hand term.

Incorporating these changes into (4.7), (4.8), and (4.12) produces:

$$P^o_t = c_0 + (c_1-c_2)P^s_{t-1} + c_2 P_{t-1} + c_3 H_{t-1}$$
$$+ c_4 U_{t-1} + (c_5-c_6)\mu^s_t + c_6 \mu_t + w \tag{4.18}$$

$$P^s_t = d_0 + (d_1-d_2)P^s_{t-1} + d_2 P_{t-1} + d_3 H_{t-1}$$
$$+ d_4 U_{t-1} + (d_5-d_6)\mu^s_t + d_6 \mu_t + w' \tag{4.19}$$

$$P_t = n_0 + (n_1-n_2)P^s_{t-1} + n_2 P_{t-1} + n_3 H_{t-1}$$
$$+ n_4 U_{t-1} + (n_5-n_6)\mu^s_t + n_6 \mu_t + w'' \tag{4.20}$$

3. Progress has been made, but there are still the unobservable P^s_{t-1} and μ^s_t terms to dispose of. Additional simplification would be possible if some relation could be deduced between the $(c_1 - c_2)$ and $(c_5 - c_6)$ terms—and, similarly of course, for the corresponding d_i and n_i terms. Here Belsley develops an ingenious assumption.[17]

First, the effect is examined of a one unit increase in lagged production to stock, P^s_{t-1}, and in current expectations of sales from stock, μ^s_t, but leaving *total* lagged production and sales expectations unchanged. It is the latter point which provides the phrase used to describe this step as one in which "no weak aggregation effects" are shown.

If one unit increases in P^s_{t-1} and μ^s_t do not affect the values of P_{t-1} and μ_t, then obviously there must be compensating one unit decreases in P^o_{t-1} and μ^o_t. And, the one unit $(+/-)$ changes described *do* cause some change in P^s_t and P^o_t—let us say a change of "m." It is then easily shown, from (4.10), that:

$$(d_1 - d_2) + (d_5 - d_6) = m. \tag{4.21}$$

Similarly,

$$(c_1 - c_2) + (c_5 - c_6) = -m. \tag{4.22}$$

and, by addition,

$$(n_1 - n_2) + (n_5 - n_6) = 0. \tag{4.23}$$

The latter relation enables combination of the P_{t-1}^s and μ_t^s terms of equation (4.20), so that we can write:

$$P_t = n_0 + (n_1 - n_2)(P_{t-1}^s - \mu_t^s) + n_2 P_{t-1}$$
$$+ n_3 H_{t-1} + n_4 U_{t-1} + n_6 \mu_t + w''. \tag{4.24}$$

4. However, corresponding treatment of (4.18) and (4.19) depends on the value of m; and, in fact, m = 1 will be required. To determine whether this would be a reasonable assumption, we adopt Belsley's tactic of using results generated within the study as a yardstick.[18]

The argument to be followed here has three steps: (a) examination of the values of the coefficients of the explanatory variables which were obtained in chapter 3, for industries *producing to stock;* (b) considering the merits of the assumption that the production to stock function, of industries producing both to order and stock, would have similar characteristics to those of (a); and (c) definition of any additional supporting information needed to support assumption.

Referring to (4.8), the precursor of (4.19), we can see that the "own effects" coefficients for P_{t-1}^s and μ_t^s for production to stock, P_t^s are d_1 and d_5. Their counterparts in equation (3.9) were d_1 and d_3; and the latters' values were given in table 1. Here, we are interested only in the values given for the four industries *not* accumulating unfilled orders (i.e., producing only to stock). And, in fact, the particular information in which we are interested is the sum of d_1 and d_3 for each of the four industries—for convenience, these are listed below:

Industry Number	$d_1 + d_3$
20	1.0889
21	1.0786
28	1.0380
39	1.0396

The sums are slightly in excess of unity in each case, and therefore, it would not seem unreasonable to expect the sums of d_1 and d_5 (in 4.19) to show similar behavior for the production to stock function of industries producing both to stock and order. If, in addition, the sums of d_2 and d_6 were found to be small and positive,[19] a glance at (4.21) shows that it would be plausible to expect m $\sim$ 1.

Using the assumption that m = 1 enables combination of the P_{t-1}^s and μ_t^s terms of (4.18) and (4.19) in a manner similar to (4.24). However, there is the difference that replacement of the $(d_5 - d_6)$ term with $1 - (d_1 - d_2)$ leaves a μ_t^s term[20] on the right-hand side of (4.19), and a similar, but negative term in (4.18). To make easier the following of the argument, the resultant equations are shown below:

$$P_t^o = c_0 + (c_1 - c_2)\,(P_{t-1}^s - \mu_t^s) + c_2 P_{t-1}$$
$$+ c_3 H_{t-1} + c_4 U_{t-1} - \mu_t^s + c^6 \mu_t + w. \tag{4.25}$$

$$P_t^s = d_0 + (d_1 - d_2)\,(P_{t-1}^s - \mu_t^s) + d_2 P_{t-1}$$
$$+ d_3 H_{t-1} + d_4 U_{t-1} - \mu_t^s + d^6 \mu_t + w'. \tag{4.26}$$

The presence of the μ_t^s term in the latter equations creates the opportunity to transform the dependent variables of (4.25) and (4.26) into observable entities. To demonstrate, addition of μ_t^s to both sides of (4.25) removes the term from the right-hand side, while the left becomes: $P_t^o + \mu_t^s$. Since $P_t^o = S_t^o$ (from 4.4) and $\mu_t^s = S_t^s - \epsilon_t$ (from 4.15), we see that:

$$P_t^o + \mu_t^s = S_t^o + S_t^s - \epsilon_t = S_t - \epsilon_t;$$

and (4.25) has become:

$$S_t = c_0 + (c_1 - c_2)\,(P_{t-1}^s - \mu_t^s) + c_2 P_{t-1}$$
$$+ c_3 H_{t-1} + c_4 U_{t-1} + c_6 \mu_t + v.^{21} \tag{4.27}$$

A corresponding change is made in (4.26) by subtraction of μ_t^s from both sides, which from (4.1), converts the dependent variable to ΔH_t.

$$\Delta H_t = d_0 + (d_1 - d_2)\,(P_{t-1}^s - \mu_t^s) + d_2 P_{t-1}$$
$$+ d_3 H_{t-1} + d_4 U_{t-1} + d_6 \mu_t + w.^{21} \tag{4.28}$$

5. At this point, we have three similar equations with c, d, and n coefficients: (4.27), (4.28), and (4.24), in which the dependent variables and all but two of the terms $(P_{t-1}^s - \mu_t^s)$, and μ_t, are available from the data. The latter poses no problem, for we can use N_t (new orders) as an unbiased estimator of expectations.

The $(P_{t-1}^s - \mu_t^s)$ term is less tractable. Belsley's solution was to accept the assumption that last period's actual sales (S_{t-1}^s) are what manufacturers producing to stock will expect to sell during the current period—i.e., *approximation by naive expectations*. The attraction of this step is that it allows replacement of the troublesome term because: $\Delta H_{t-1} = P_{t-1}^s - S_{t-1}^s$ (from 4.1). This is the final link in the chain, and the three equations can now be transformed into the testable models below:

$$S_t = c_0 + (c_1 - c_2)\Delta H_{t-1} + c_2 P_{t-1} + c_3 H_{t-1}$$
$$+ c_4 U_{t-1} + c_6 \mu_t + v. \tag{4.29}$$

$$\Delta H_t = d_0 + (d_1 - d_2)\Delta H_{t-1} + d_2 P_{t-1} + d_3 H_{t-1}$$
$$+ d_4 U_{t-1} + d_6 \mu_t + w'. \tag{4.30}$$

$$P_t = n_0 + (n_1 - n_2)\Delta H_{t-1} + n_2 P_{t-1} + n_3 H_{t-1}$$
$$+ n_4 U_{t-1} + n_6 \mu_t + w''. \tag{4.31}$$

To recapitulate briefly, the merits of these models are:

1. Equation (4.31) represents the profit-maximizing level of overall production when there is production *both* to stock and order.

2. The manner of derivation means that the c_i and d_i coefficients of (4.29) and (4.30) are the same coefficients which appeared in (4.7) and (4.8), the original structural expressions for P_t^o and P_t^s, respectively. However, numerical estimates for P_t^o and P_t^s cannot be calculated from these relations (because of the unobservable variable terms in the latter pair of equations).

3. The "own effects" coefficients of (4.30) (d_1, d_3, and d_5) correspond by derivation to the coefficients of a structural model for production to stock only. Similarly, for (4.29), c_2, c_4, and c_6 represent "own effects" for production to order.

However, there are three criticisms to be made which detract from (but do not invalidate) the final result. Two of these stem from the final "sales expectations by naive approximation" assumption made above.

1. The assumption of $N_{t-1}^s = \mu_t^s$ is at odds with the initial assumption in the derivation of a testable model, namely,

$$N_t^s \equiv S_t^s = \mu_t^s + \epsilon_t. \tag{4.15}$$

Results from the present study, which are presented in chapter 7, lend strong support to (4.15). The evidence is good that manufacturers to stock accurately estimate next period's actual sales.

2. The second criticism is along the following lines.

  The differential between two period's sales (for sales from stock) can be written:

$$DS_t^s = S_t^s - S_{t-1}^s,$$

or

$$S_{t-1}^s = S_t^s - DS_t^s.$$

This means that the "naive expectations" approximation, which uses S_{t-1}^s, instead of S_t^s, as the estimate for μ_t^s, understates actual sales by precisely DS_t^s. Unfortunately, the latter term is not separately available from the census data. DSP_t would be, of course, but not its component "to stock" part, so correction cannot be made.

  Later in this study, it will be demonstrated that the covariance between DS_t and DP_t for production to stock industries is close to unity. From this observation, therefore, comes the inference that the several cost-minimizing production levels defined by these decision rules tend to be understated by $\sim(c_1 - c_2)DS^S$—(or the corresponding term using d_i or n_i).

  The third criticism is related to assumption (4), which was that the value of (m) could be interpreted as m = 1. This assumption has a built-in distortion, which is difficult to quantify, but whose effects can at least be suggested.

  Table 1 showed that by far the largest coefficient for each of the four industries producing only to stock (i.e., Industries 20, 21, 28, and 29) was the coefficient of μ_t (or its proxy, N_t). In each case, its standard error was smaller than that of any of the other coefficients; and, in other words, well and away in each case, the coefficient of μ_t was the most significant.

  A partial equation (from 4.19) would be helpful here, while considering the m = 1 assumption:

$$P_t^s = (d_1 - d_2) \cdot P_{t-1}^s + (d_5 - d_6) \cdot \mu_t^s + \dots \quad .$$

For simplification, we could call this relation of the form:

$$P_t^s = a \cdot P_{t-1}^s + b \cdot \mu_t^s + \dots \quad ,$$

and the adoption of m = 1 is equivalent to accepting b = (1−a), so that in effect we would have:

$$P_t^s = a \cdot P_{t-1}^s + (1 - a)\mu_t^s + \dots \quad .$$

The difference in value between (1–a) and (b) as the coefficients for any industry would be an empirical matter. But, to the extent that $(1-a) \neq b$, the model has suffered a distortion in value for the largest, and most significant, of its coefficients. Unfortunately, the nonseparability of the sales to order, and the sale to stock data, for industries which produce to both, means that the observation cannot be quantified. It remains true that the data examined did reasonably support the premise that $m \sim 1$, and therefore the distortion may be accepted as a matter of degree rather than of disqualification.

This relatively minor drift from the bull's eye is not a serious problem, however—particularly if it can be specifically identified in advance as it has been here. As the results of chapter 5 will show, the overall performance of Belsley's empirical models (in terms of closely fitting the statistical data, and in allowing additional useful inferences) is extremely good.

5

Testing the Models

The results of regression tests on the models developed in the last chapter for production to stock, and for production to both stock and order, are evaluated in this chapter. In addition to results observed directly, there are inferences made on points which will be explored in detail in succeeding chapters.

First, the results of OLSQ regression tests are given of Bureau of Census data for the 1958–1976 period on the four industries included in this study, which produce only to stock. The model, repeated below as (5.1), is the same as used earlier (in chapter 3).

$$P_t = d_0 + d_1 P_{t-1} + d_2 H_{t-1} + d_3 \mu_t + \epsilon_t \tag{5.1}$$

New orders have been used again as a proxy for sales expectations, μ_t.

The evaluations were made using both quarterly and monthly lengths of period, and using both seasonally adjusted and nonadjusted data, so that there are four sets of results altogether. These are reported on: table 2—quarterly, seasonally adjusted; table 3—quarterly, nonadjusted; table 4—monthly, seasonally adjusted; and table 5—monthly, nonadjusted.

Overall, the results are excellent. It is obvious from the R^2 values that the sets of data fit the model closely. The principal explanatory variable is clearly sales expectations, or its proxy, new orders. (Coefficients significant at the 1 percent level are marked **, and at the 5 percent level, *, on the tables.) The d_3 coefficients are all significant at the 1 percent level. Most of the d_0 and d_2 coefficients are significant at the 5 percent level or better, and almost half of the d_1's.

Before undertaking a detailed analysis of the test results, however, it will be in order to examine the data and the models for evidence of, and difficulties caused by, autocorrelation—or any other attendant problems. Table 6 shows a comparison of the Durbin-Watson test results (from tables 2-5), and the theoretical test values for first order autocorrelation.

The results were generally in the 1.12–1.97 range.[1] Of the four industries, tobacco (number 21) is the only one to show essentially no tendency toward (first order) autocorrelation. That one of the four does not, is, of itself, a minor

Table 2. Regression Results for Industries Producing to Stock,
Quarterly Data, Seasonally Adjusted

$$P_t = d_0 + d_1 P_{t-1} + d_2 H_{t-1} + d_3 N_t + \varepsilon_t$$

Ind.		d_0	d_1	d_2	d_3	$\bar{R}^2$ / F Stat.	Std. Error of Regres.	Mean of Depen. Var.	Durbin Watson Stat.
20	Coef.	158.1*	.0122	-0.304**	1.043**	.9997			
	(Std. error)	(68.1)	(.0306)	(.068)	(.026)		163	25,061	1.7572
	t stat.	2.32	.400	-4.49	40.3	93,852			
21	Coef.	-53.8*	-.0335	-0.163*	1.097**	.9925			
	(Std. error)	(22.2)	(.0684)	(.067)	(.068)		28.9	1,363	1.9719
	t stat.	-2.42	-.489	-2.44	16.2	3,172			
28	Coef.	43.0	.125**	-0.217**	0.926**	.9998			
	(Std. error)	(25.1)	(.021)	(.033)	(.019)		80.9	12,526	1.226
	t stat.	1.71	5.85	-6.58	48.7	144,473			
29	Coef.	274**	.0183	-0.397**	1.014**	.9999			
	(Std. error)	(62.1)	(.0208)	(.085)	(.017)		57.4	7,841	1.5230
	t stat.	4.41	.88	-4.67	58.5	225,433			

*Indicates coefficients significant at the 5 percent level.

**Indicates coefficients significant at the 1 percent level.

Table 3. Regression Results for Industries Producing to Stock, Quarterly Data, Nonadjusted

$$P_t = d_0 + d_1 P_{t-1} + d_2 H_{t-1} + d_3 N_t + \varepsilon_t$$

Ind.		d_0	d_1	d_2	d_3	R^2 / F Stat.	Std. Error of Regres.	Mean of Depen. Var.	Durbin Watson Stat.
20	Coef.	315.1**	.00185	-.511**	1.087**	.9994			
	(Std. error)	(102.9)	(.0433)	(.102)	(.0342)		256.4	25,053	1.6128
	t stat.	3.06	.043	-5.02	31.8	37,747			
21	Coef.	-67.1**	.0756	-0.211**	1.003**	.9906			
	(Std. error)	(25.7)	(.0565)	(.077)	(.056)		32.5	1,362	2.1114
	t stat.	-2.61	1.34	-2.74	17.8	2,520			
28	Coef.	38.5	.0670**	-0.156**	0.971**	.9995			
	(Std. error)	(44.6)	(.0225)	(.056)	(.021)		144.2	12,539	1.8151
	t stat.	.864	2.96	-2.78	46.2	46,198			
29	Coef.	394.5**	.0196	-0.543**	1.020**	.9998			
	(Std. error)	(78.1)	(.0258)	(.105)	(.021)		71.5	7,842	1.6541
	t stat.	5.05	.763	-5.17	48.2	145,309			

*Indicates coefficients significant at the 5 percent level.

**Indicates coefficients significant at the 1 percent level.

Table 4. Regression Results for Industries Producing to Stock, Monthly Data, Seasonally Adjusted

$$P_t = d_0 + d_1 P_{t-1} + d_2 H_{t-1} + d_3 N_t + \varepsilon_t$$

Ind.		d_0	d_1	d_2	d_3	$\bar{R}^2$ / F Stat.	Std. Error of Regres.	Mean of Depen. Var.	Durbin Watson Stat.
20	Coef.	45.2*	.0664*	-0.098**	0.988**	.9993			
	(Std. error)	(20.5)	(.0262)	(.019)	(.025)		90.6	8,296	1.7161
	t stat.	2.21	2.54	-5.15	39.1	103,188			
21	Coef.	-19.9*	-0.038	-0.071**	1.112**	.9618			
	(Std. error)	(8.74)	(.053)	(.027)	(.055)		21.9	452	2.3523
	t stat.	-2.28	-.71	-2.62	20.3	1,915			
28	Coef.	7.48	.204**	-0.047**	0.832**	.9995			
	(Std. error)	(7.89)	(.026)	(.0010)	(.025)		45.1	4,135	2.3216
	t stat.	.95	7.92	-4.73	33.0	158,548			
29	Coef.	81.3**	.0302	-0.119**	0.999**	.9997			
	(Std. error)	(18.8)	(.025)	(.025)	(.024)		30.5	2,591	1.6856
	t stat.	432	1.21	-4.72	42.3	268,551			

*Indicates coefficients significant at the 5 percent level.

**Indicates coefficients significant at the 1 percent level.

Table 5. Regression Results for Industries Producing to Stock, Monthly Data, Nonadjusted

$$P_t = d_0 + d_1 P_{t-1} + d_2 H_{t-1} + d_3 N_t + \epsilon_t$$

Ind.		d_0	d_1	d_2	d_3	$\bar{R}^2$ / F Stat.		Std. Error of Regres.	Mean of Depen. Var.	Durbin Watson Stat.
20	Coef.	88.0**	.0867**	-0.166**	1.002**	.9985		128.3	8,292	1.1227
	(Std. error)	(27.4)	(.0261)	(.0230)	(.0246)					
	t stat.	3.21	3.33	-7.19	40.7		51,601			
21	Coef.	-27.5*	-.0016	-0.114**	1.110**	.9337		29.4	452	1.9363
	(Std. error)	(11.3)	(.057)	(.035)	(.059)					
	t stat.	-2.43	-.027	-3.30	18.9		1,071			
28	Coef.	-3.46	.0997**	-.0009	0.906**	.9992		60.7	4,141	1.1409
	(Std. error)	(10.5)	(.016)	(.012)	(.016)					
	t stat.	-.330	6.19	-.076	56.6		89,454			
29	Coef.	106.1**	.0788**	-0.149**	0.956**	.9996		35.6	2,591	1.3135
	(Std. error)	(20.8)	(.025)	(.027)	(.023)					
	t stat.	5.10	3.21	-5.48	41.3		196,975			

*Indicates coefficients significant at the 5 percent level.

**Indicates coefficients significant at the 1 percent level.

Table 6. Durbin-Watson Test Results for Industries Producing to Stock

Industry No.	Quarterly Data, Seasonally Adjusted		Quarterly Data, Nonadjusted		Monthly Data, Seasonally Adjusted		Monthly Data, Nonadjusted	
	@ 1%	@ 5%	@ 1%	@ 5%	@ 1%	@ 5%	@ 1%	@ 5%
20	no	no	no	?	no	?	yes+	yes+
21	no	no	no	no	no	?	no	no
28	yes+	yes+	no	no	no	?	yes+	yes+
29	?	yes+	no	?	no	?	yes+	yes+

Table 6 shows results of comparison of the Durbin-Watson test statistics (from Tables 2-5), d*, with d_L and d_u theoretical values at the 1 percent and 5 percent levels of significance. These values, for functions containing three explanatory variables, are:

Period	No. of Observations	at 1%		at 5%	
		d_L	d_u	d_L	d_u
Quarterly	76	1.39	1.56	1.54	1.71
Monthly	304	1.48	1.60	1.61	1.74

On the table, test results are reported as:

[a] No = d_u < d* < (4 - d_u) = null hypothesis of no autocorrelation is accepted.

[b] ? = d_L < d* < d_u or (4 - d_u) < d* < (4 - d_L) = the test is inconclusive.

[c] Yes+ = d* < d_L = null hypothesis rejected; positive first order autocorrelation accepted.

surprise, for, as Koutsoyiannis[2] remarks, "Autocorrelation is a problem specific to time series data. Due to economic growth and business cycles, autocorrelation is positive in most economic relationships." The others, particularly chemicals and petroleum (numbers 28 and 29) show themselves to be more in the spirit of the latter remark.

There are interesting differences between data periods of different length, with and without seasonal adjustment. The quarterly (unadjusted) data reflected the least indication of any tendency toward autocorrelation, while the monthly (unadjusted) results showed autocorrelation unambiguously, for three of the four industries.

With these results in mind, it is advisable to remember the effects of autocorrelation upon OLSQ regression results—i.e., that while estimates of parameter coefficients remain statistically unbiased, their variances may be seriously understated. In turn, this means their true significance might readily be less than what regression results would seem to indicate.

in which the most recent values of X have the greatest influence. If the effect of each of the previous periods were declining in some sort of geometric manner, we would have: However, there is an additional complication caused by the appearance in the test relation of P_{t-1}, a lagged term of the dependent variable. The nature of the problem posed by P_{t-1} can be illustrated with the following example. Let us consider a model:

$$Y_t = a_0 + b_0 X_t + b_1 X_{t-1} + b_2 X_{t-2} + \ldots p\, u_t,$$

$b_1 = \lambda b_0$, $b_2 = \lambda^2 b_0$, and, in general, $b_i = \lambda^i b_0$ with $(0 < \lambda < 1)$. This of course, is the type of model brought to attention by Koyck. Use of the Koyck transformation with such a model enables its conversion to the form (ignoring, for simplicity, the a_0 term) of: $Y_t = b_0 X_t + \lambda Y_{t-1} + v_t$. While the greater convenience afforded by the latter expression might be the usual purpose of such an operation, our present attention is directed at the resulting effects upon the error term. It can readily be shown that the new error term, v_t, is expressed: $v_t = u_t - \lambda u_{t-1}$. And, the resultant error term is autocorrelated, even though the original u_t term had not been.

The problem may be viewed in several ways. If, as is fairly likely (given the characteristics of time series variables), the X's of the original relationship represented a collinear pattern, the effects of the collinearity are now expressed in the error term. Or, the matter could be approached from the standpoint of the independence (or lack of it) of a lagged variable term from the error term, for independence is one of assumptions underlying standard regression analysis. Clearly, to the extent that the Y_{t-1} term can be "explained" (or replaced by) a series of X_{t-i} terms, a connection is signalled between the error and the lagged variable term. And the point has been illustrated of why the presence of a lagged endogenous term in a model is an early warning signal of potential autocorrelation difficulties.

Griliches[3] has found that OLS estimates of coefficients are no longer asymptotically unbiased, under these circumstances, leading to their overestimation. Nerlove and Wallis[4] have reported also that the Durbin-Watson test statistic, "d," tends to be biased toward a value of 2, in the presence of the lagged dependent variable term (thus tending to understate autocorrelation actually present). However, Koutsoyiannis'[5] remarks that, "This finding has alarmed econometricians unduly, because the bias of d (towards 2) is serious for models containing only Y_{t-1}. Malinvaud has shown that the bias in d tends to decrease if apart from Y_{t-1} there are exogenous X's in the model."

At this point, of course, we are led to consider how estimates of these coefficients might be improved. It would be possible, for instance, to calculate new, more efficient estimates of the regression parameters, by using the Durbin procedure of: (1) estimating the value of ρ, the autocorrelation coefficient; (2) using the estimate, $\hat{\rho}$, to transform the variable data of the test relation; (3) and, to apply OLSQ to the transformed data to provide new estimates of the parameters. Before embarking on this approach, however, there is yet another problem to consider.

The explanatory variables of test relation (5.1) are N_t, P_{t-1}, and H_{t-1}. The correlation coefficients of $N_t:P_{t-1}$ (as derived from monthly, nonadjusted data, 1958–1976) are listed below:

Industry 20	.989
Industry 21	.902
Industry 28	.984
Industry 29	.997

Similarly, for the correlation coefficients of $N_t:H_{t-1}$:

Industry 20	.970
Industry 21	.860
Industry 28	.953
Industry 29	.973

Given the close correlation existing between the explanatory variables, we can assume (close to) linear relations between the variables, and hence a close approach to multicollinearity.

When multicollinearity exists,[6] "it becomes very difficult to obtain precise estimates of the *separate* effects of the variables involved." Values for the estimated coefficients can be very sensitive to addition or deletion of a few observations. A not uncommon problem which arises is that coefficients do not appear significantly different from zero, this leading to the conclusion that a particular variable should be dropped from (or not included in) the analysis, not

> because they have no effect, but simply because the (observed) sample is inadequate to isolate the effect precisely. This result obtains despite possibly high $\bar{R}^2$ or "F values" indicating "significant" explanatory power of the model.

Let us consider the above in the light of an empirical experimenter trying to develop a model which would explain the production decision for a firm manufacturing to stock. The simplest possible relation would be:

$$P_t = d \cdot \mu_t + \epsilon_t \tag{5.2}$$

If this were tested with monthly, unadjusted, data for 1958–1976, the results shown in table 7 would be obtained.

Table 7.   OLSQ Regression Test of a Simple Model

	Ind. 20	Ind. 21	Ind. 28	Ind. 29
Value of d	1.0031	1.0029	1.0042	1.0029
Standard error	(.0010)	(.0042)	(.0003)	(.0008)
$\underline{t}$ statistic	962	237	1,081	1,258
$\bar{R}^2$	.9982	.9308	.9990	.9996
Std. error of regression	141.5	29.9	65.2	38.2
Mean of dependent variable	8,292	452	4,141	2,591

NOTE: $P_t = d \cdot N_t + \epsilon_t$.

For simplification, we will omit here the "normal next steps" of trying out other possible variables. (Hopefully, these would, for the theoretical reasons of chapter 4, include P_{t-1} and H_{t-1}, and, of course a constant term. Other plausible choices abound.) We turn to comparison of table 7 with the regression results of table 5, which included the variables just mentioned. There is microscopic benefit in the $\bar{R}^2$'s in three cases (e.g., from .9990 to .9992 for Industry 28) and none at all for Industry 29. The "t" statistics for the additional coefficients are significant in nine cases, but two of them are not for Industry 28, and a different one not for Industry 29.

Depending on the method and logic used, it is clear that the ultimate decision on what constituted "a proper model" could vary. In addition, of course, which industries were under study, and what observation period was used represent additional variability in the final decision.

The present study does not have this problem. The variables in the relation under examination are present by derivation, a priori, from a cost-minimization standpoint. A good fit with the data can be interpreted as confirmation that profit-maximizing behavior has been shown. The data series employed do have strongly collinear characteristics. However, appreciation of this fact and the ways in which least square regressions might be affected suffices for our purposes—further remedial steps are not required.

Returning, with this in mind, to the earlier question on the merits of using the Durbin (or other) technique to obtain "better estimates" of the parameter coefficients, the answer is that real benefit is questionable for the following reasons:

1. The purpose of the regression tests (reported on tables 2–5) has been to confirm (or reject) the acceptability of the hypothesis that firms/industries produce on a profit-maximizing basis.[7] So far in our interpretation, they do.

2. If it were also intended to use the coefficients for predictive purpose, a case could be made for "better efficiency." Econometric projections, however, are not the purpose. Nor, do the further analytical needs of this paper require "refinement" of the coefficients.

3. In any case, the greater the collinearity of the data base, the less dependence should be placed on individual coefficients, whether or not adjusted by a two-stage regression technique.

We can turn now to: (1) interpretation of the coefficients, (2) comparison of quarterly vs. monthly, and seasonally adjusted vs. unadjusted data series, and, (3) inter-industry differences in characteristics.

Interpretation of the Coefficients: Production to Stock

The d_1, d_2, and d_3 coefficients of equation (5.1) represent the increment to be made to the cost-minimizing level of production for the current period for each one unit ceteris paribus change in P_{t-1}, H_{t-1}, and μ_t respectively. From their derivation, outlined in chapter 3, we would expect their numerical values to lie between 0 and 1; d_2 should be negative, and also $d_2 = -d_3$.

d_1 is based on the costs of changing production level. A value near 1 would imply that a current production level was indicated of similar size to last period's—i.e., that there are substantial costs to changing the rate of production. A value near zero implies the opposite.

d_2 is expected to be negative. The conventional explanation is that a larger stock of finished goods on hand means less production required in the current period. However, it is more in the spirit of chapter 3 to use an alternate explanation—that the larger the costs of holding inventory, the lower will be the cost-minimizing level of current production *for inventory*. Extending the alternate explanation (and noting from derivation that $d_2 = -d_3$) the notion is expressed that the less production for inventory, the more production for sales.[8] And, of course, the larger are current sales expectations, the larger the amount of current production called for.

However, the length of the time period in the data used plays an important role because H_t is a *stock* quantity, while P_t and S_t are *flows*. It makes a considerable computational difference when comparing magnitudes of H_t and S_t, whether the latter represents a day's sale, a week's sale, a month's, or a year's. After all, sales for a given day might well be only ~0.3 percent of the annual figure. On the other hand, the stock on hand on a given date is unaffected by the length of preceding period chosen. Therefore, conceptually we can realize that a time period exists for which the magnitudes of H_{t-1} and μ_t would be such that $d_2 = -d_3$. However, there is no a priori reason to expect that this time period[9] (for any particular industry) would in fact turn out to be a month, or a quarter. And, these being the periods utilized in the study, we must relax the $d_2 = -d_3$ assumption.

Therefore, we expect d_3 simply to indicate the degree to which current sales expectations affect the production decision. A value of ~1.0 would imply that manufacturers attempt to closely match current production to current sales expectations. How successful their efforts are in this direction will be investigated in chapter 7.

The next task is to compare the results obtained with quarterly and monthly data (seasonally adjusted or not) to establish which type and period is most useful.

From an overall view of the results of tables 2–5, it can be seen that use of quarterly data (vs. monthly data) results in higher $\bar{R}^2$'s and lower standard errors of regression. Seasonally adjusted (X–9) data have similar merits when compared with nonadjusted data. Can we conclude that QS (quarterly, seasonally adjusted) is the preferable choice for a study of this type?

Actually, there is good reason to argue that M (monthly, nonadjusted) data are preferable. With the exception of Industry 21 (which shows maverick tendencies from time to time), the $\bar{R}^2$ values for M data are really still extremely good. And, the $\bar{R}^2$'s derived from monthly data, and from quarterly data, for an industry are not, strictly speaking, comparable. Zellner and Mont-marquette[10] have investigated the effects on regression testing of time series data models using more, or less, temporally aggregated data (e.g., use of quarterly vs. monthly data). They report the more aggregated data will generally produce results in which the error terms are autocorrelated in a fashion akin to those obtained with a moving average process. Then, purely as a mathematical effect, the $\bar{R}^2$'s of the quarterly data will be larger than the corresponding results obtained from the monthly set, and the difference is not to be construed as an improvement in fit.

Their conclusion reminds us again, that ideally, choice of time period should be based on a priori consideration reflecting such factors as, e.g., speed of response to changes. In the present case, use of monthly data (as will later be demonstrated) is preferable to quarterly for just this reason.

The next question is whether seasonally adjusted data are to be preferred to unadjusted data. We note that the seasonally adjusted data of tables 2 and 4 show a small superiority, in terms of $\bar{R}^2$'s, to those of tables 3 and 5. However, as outlined above, moving average smoothing (which is precisely the seasonal adjustment process) tends to create spuriously higher $\bar{R}^2$'s.

There are two additional reasons to prefer the unadjusted data:

1. From a purely mechanical standpoint, more coefficients can be counted as significant at the 1 percent level from "unadjusted" results than for "seasonally adjusted." (No difference in the number of coefficients significant at 5 percent.)

2. From a more practical point of view, seasonally adjusted data, of itself, actually abstracts from the month-to-month decision process faced by managers.

On balance, therefore, monthly data appear preferable to quarterly, and unadjusted data to seasonally adjusted. Consequently, interpretive emphasis after this chapter will be put on monthly unadjusted data. Some data series, in particular, the Federal Trade Commission (FTC) Quarterly Report, are not available monthly (as betrayed by the title). Where monthly data are not available, second choice will be for quarterly, unadjusted data series.

Before turning to inter-industry comparisons, one final point can be developed. The earlier discussion concerning the consequences of autocorrelation and collinearity cast a shadow on the dependability of the coefficients reported in tables 2–5. It would be convenient if there were some external yardstick against which they could be measured—but, there is none. However, there is one internally generated measuring device available.

Since the flow magnitudes, represented by the other variables, are approximately three times larger for quarterly data than for monthly, it would be reasonable to expect d_2 to be ~$3\times$ larger in the former case, if the relation between H_{t-1} and the other variables is to be maintained. The monthly d_2 for

Industry 28 is not a significant result and will not be used; but, all the remaining monthly and quarterly d_2's are significant at the 1 percent level. None of the quarterly d_2's, for the other three industries, is precisely $3\times$ the corresponding monthly d_2;[11] but the range of the quarterly/monthly ratio is 1.85–3.64, and, the mean is 2.86, with standard deviation of .92. The implication would be that individual coefficients are not precisely correct, but overall, in the ballpark.

Inter-Industry Comparisons: Production to Stock

For convenience in the following exposition, quarterly and monthly data (unadjusted) will be denoted by Q and M. Seasonally adjusted data, by QS and MS.

Similarities in the results were more pronounced than inter-industry differences. The $\bar{R}^2$ terms for each industry on tables 2–5 were all .99++, indicative of close fits with the data, except for Industry 21. The latter's fit with QS data ($\bar{R}^2 = .9925$) was close, not as good with MS or Q data, and furthest from the mark (thought still reasonable, $\bar{R}^2 = .9337$) with M. All d_1, d_2, and d_3 coefficients had the signs expected, except for the d_1 of Industry 21, which was negative three times out of four (with none of the four found significant).

In all cases, the most important variable in determining optimum production level was current sales expectations. All d_3 coefficients were significant at the 1 percent level, and generally, $d_3 \sim 1.0$. Next most important was the coefficient of H_{t-1}, which generally was the next largest coefficient, and only once was a d_2 nonsignificant (at least at the 5 percent level).

To summarize, the production level for the forthcoming period appears determined mainly by sales expectations. This, together with the generally small but positive coefficients for P_{t-1}, which signifies a relatively small cost to changing the rate of production, suggests that *production for these industries conforms closely to actual sales.* Just how closely is explored in chapter 6.

Production to both Order and Stock

The profit-maximizing levels of production for industries producing to both order and stock were derived in chapter 4, as equations (4.7) and (4.8). They are repeated below for convenience.

$$P_t^o = c_0 + c_1 P_{t-1}^s + c_2 P_{t-1}^o + c_3 H_{t-1}$$
$$+ c_4 U_{t-1} + c_5 \mu_t^s + c_6 \mu_t^o + e_t. \tag{5.3}$$

$$P_t^s = d_0 + d_1 P_{t-1}^s + d_2 P_{t-1}^o + d_3 H_{t-1}$$
$$+ d_4 U_{t-1} + d_5 \mu_t^s + d_6 \mu_t^o + e_t'. \tag{5.4}$$

These relationships cannot be tested directly because data are not observable for all the factors; but testable expressions were derived from which the coefficients of the two equations can be determined (i.e., 4.29, 4.30, and 4.31). It is the objective of this portion of the analysis to examine the numerical results and significance of the coefficients for equations (5.3) and (5.4), which have been derived from the results of testing (4.29), (4.30), and (4.31).

OLSQ regressions were performed on the latter three equations, for Industries 26, 27, 34, 35, and 36, using Bureau of Census data for 1958–1976. Both monthly and quarterly, and seasonally adjusted and nonadjusted, series were employed. The results obtained for (4.29) and (4.30) closely paralleled those reported at the beginning of the chapter in ranges of $\bar{R}^2$'s, standard errors, and Durbin-Watson statistics. Because of their similarity (and bulk), presentation of these results and repetition of the earlier discussion regarding tendencies toward, and problems caused by, serial correlation are considered unnecessary.

In the case of (4.31), the dependent variable is the first difference term, ΔH_t, and, as a consequence, the $\bar{R}^2$'s obtained were relatively low. However, the standard errors of regression corresponded in magnitude to the first two relations sufficiently well to confirm acceptability of the results. Once again, new orders have been used as the proxy for sales expectations. The relation of N_t, new orders, to sales, S_t, is:

$$N_t^s = S_t^s$$

$$\frac{N_t^o = S_t^o + \Delta U_t}{N_t = S_t + \Delta U_t} \tag{5.5}$$

where $\Delta U_t = U_t - U_{t-1}$. Translation of the coefficients from the regression-tested relations, into (5.3) and (5.4) is straightforward, for c_0, c_2, c_3, c_4, c_6, and their d_i counterparts. The c_1's and d_1's are available from the difference terms, $(c_1 - c_2)$ and $(d_1 - d_2)$; and, finally, c_5 and d_5 from their derivation in chapter 4, wherein:

$$(c_1 - c_2) + (c_5 - c_6) = -1,$$

and,

$$(d_1 - d_2) + (d_5 - d_6) = 1.$$

The results of the evaluation of the coefficients for equations (5.3) and (5.4) are presented in tables 8–15, as summarized below: table 8—coefficients for P_t^o, data, quarterly, seasonally adjusted; table 9—coefficients for P_t^o, data, quarterly nonadjusted; table 10—coefficients for P_t^o, data, monthly,

Table 8. Estimated Coefficients for Industries with Unfilled Orders: Production to Order. Quarterly Data, Seasonally Adjusted

Ind. No.	$P_t^O = c_0 + c_1 P_{t-1}^S + c_2 P_{t-1}^O + c_3 H_{t-1} + c_4 U_{t-1} + c_5 N_t^S + c_6 N_t^O$						
	c_0	c_1	c_2	c_3	c_4	c_6	c_6
26	-2.91	-.099	.176**	-.054	.216**	.076	.801**
	(13.6)	(.183)	(.031)	(.081)	(.081)	(.218)	(.026)
27	-.472	-.004	.063*	.020	.034	.000	.933**
	(17.0)	(.113)	(.031)	(.090)	(.042)	(.126)	(.028)
34	157	-1.191**	.365**	.646**	.028	1.028**	.472**
	(91)	(.283)	(.065)	(.097)	(.018)	(.283)	(.041)
35	-93.1	-.803*	.715**	.201	.013	.752	.234**
	(116)	(.365)	(.050)	(.106)	(.013)	.389	(.027)
36	56.9	-.430	.459**	.612**	.024	.278	.389**
	(66)	(.370)	(.071)	(.160)	(.021)	(.392)	(.038)

NOTE: Standard errors in parentheses.

SOURCE: Bureau of Census: Manufacturers' Shipments, Inventories, and Orders (1958-1976); quarterly, seasonally adjusted.

*Indicates coefficients significant at the 5 percent level.

**Indicates coefficients significant at the 1 percent level.

seasonally adjusted; table 11—coefficients for P_t^O, data, monthly, nonadjusted; table 12—coefficients for P_t^S, data, quarterly, seasonally adjusted; table 13—coefficients for P_t^S, data, quarterly, nonadjusted; table 14—coefficients for P_t^S, data, monthly, seasonally adjusted; and table 15— coefficients for P_t^S, data, monthly, nonadjusted. Under each coefficient (in parenthesis) is its standard error. Coefficients significant at the 5 percent level, by standard two-tailed "t" test, are marked (*), and 1 percent level (**).

Interpretation of Coefficients: Production to both Order and Stock

Before inspection of the test results, however, it would be well to review what we might expect to see.

These relations have some unusual characteristics. They separately represent levels of production for industries accumulating unfilled orders (i.e., producing to both stock and order) for production to order, P_t^O, and for production to stock, P_t^S, which have been derived from linear decision, profit-maximizing rules. They cannot be directly verified, because P_t^O and P_t^S are not

Table 9.   Estimated Coefficients for Industries with Unfilled Orders:
Production to Order. Quarterly Data, Nonadjusted

Ind. No.	$P_t^o = c_0 + c_1 P_{t-1}^s + c_2 P_{t-1}^o + c_3 H_{t-1} + c_4 U_{t-1} + c_5 N_t^s + c_6 N_t^o$						
	c_0	c_1	c_2	c_3	c_4	c_5	c_6
26	-5.23	-.243**	.190**	-.005	.299**	.200*	.767**
	(12.3)	(.092)	(.023)	(.072)	(.068)	(.092)	(.016)
27	-5.73	-.029	.016	.054	.059	.018	.973**
	(19.9)	(.111)	(.014)	(.099)	(.050)	(.109)	(.015)
34	288*	-.790**	.172*	.849**	.041	.554*	.592**
	(129)	(.305)	(.076)	(.127)	(.024)	(.270)	(.046)
35	-271	1.054	.507**	.807**	.002	-1.245*	.302**
	301	(.575)	(.099)	(.249)	(.003)	(.594)	(.049)
36	18.9	-1.642**	.302**	.723**	.066*	1.417**	.473**
	(100)	(.277)	(.075)	(.211)	(.031)	(.289)	(.046)

NOTE: Standard errors in parentheses.

SOURCE: Bureau of Census: Manufacturers' Shipments, Inventories, and Orders (1958-1976); quarterly, nonadjusted.

*Indicates coefficients significant at the 5 percent level.

**Indicates coefficients significant at the 1 percent level.

separately available as Bureau of Census data (nor likely to be in the future). Further, it is not possible to estimate values for P_t^o and P_t^s, not because we lack estimates of the coefficients, but because the stock vs. order portion of the new orders parameter is unknown—and, of course, the same is true of the lagged production terms. So far, this would seem a recitation of complete inadequacy.

However, their redeeming features are significant. They allow, through evaluation of "own effects," inter-industry comparison of the two different types of production—even though separate data on these functions are not available. They provide the yardstick, for verification purposes, of the "own effects" of production to stock vs. the (already examined) behavior of industries producing *only* to stock. If the results for the production to stock process, of industries accumulating unfilled orders, can be reasonably validated, then we can also reasonably suppose the production to order function, *otherwise not separately visible,* is described. And finally, we have the additional information about each industry, which can be derived from the

Table 10.   Estimated Coefficients for Industries with Unfilled Orders: Production to Order. Monthly Data, Seasonally Adjusted

Ind. No.	$P^o_t = c_0 + c_1 P^s_{t-1} + c_2 P^o_{t-1} + c_3 H_{t-1} + c_4 U_{t-1} + c_5 N^s_t + c_6 N^o_t$						
	c_0	c_1	c_2	c_3	c_4	c_5	c_6
26	3.32	-.012	.382**	.028	.085**	-.041	.565**
	(3.27)	(.064)	(.024)	(.019)	(.021)	(.077)	(.182)
27	-1.78	.003	.100**	.032	.019	-.018	.885**
	(5.36)	(.064)	(.023)	(.026)	(.013)	(.081)	(.023)
34	32.9	-.409**	.589**	.141**	.002	.312*	.314**
	(17.8)	(.129)	(.057)	(.020)	(.003)	(.128)	(.026)
35	-9.3	-.261*	.804**	.067**	.003	.202	.137**
	(19.4)	(.117)	(.027)	(.018)	(.002)	(.125)	(.015)
36	8.01	-.061	.708**	.128**	.005	-.029	.202**
	(12.2)	(.111)	(.036)	(.030)	(.004)	(.125)	(.021)

NOTE: Standard errors in parentheses.

SOURCE: Bureau of Census: Manufacturers' Shipments, Inventories, and Orders (1958-1976); monthly, seasonally adjusted.

*Indicates coefficients significant at the 5 percent level.

**Indicates coefficients significant at the 1 percent level.

"cross effects" between the production to order and production to stock functions.

In the previous chapter, which followed Belsley's[12] derivation of these particular equations, it was pointed out that the "own effects" coefficients of P^s_{t-1}, H_{t-1}, and μ^s_t (i.e., d_1, d_3, and d_5) corresponded directly to the coefficients: d_1, d_2, and d_3 of a production *only* to stock function (5.1). The range of values and signs expected are therefore the same in both cases. For c_2, c_4, and c_6, the "own coefficients" for manufacture to order, the reasoning for the coefficients accompanying P^o_{t-1}, and μ^s_t are quite parallel to their "to order" counterparts. For c_4, the coefficient of U_{t-1}, the higher are the costs of holding unfilled orders, the greater will be the amount of production called forth to reduce them— hence a positive sign expected for c_4, with the same 0,1 range.

With respect to *cross effects,* if production to order and production to stock processes were operated quite *independently* of each other, the "other" process would play no role at all in reaching forthcoming production levels.

Table 11. Estimated Coefficients for Industries with Unfilled Orders: Production to Order. Monthly Data, Nonadjusted

Ind. No.	$P^o_t = c_0 + c_1 P^s_{t-1} + c_2 P^o_{t-1} + c_3 H_{t-1} + c_4 U_{t-1} + c_5 N^s_t + c_6 N^o_t$						
	c_0	c_1	c_2	c_3	c_4	c_5	c_6
26	8.61 (5.3)	-.119 (.084)	.129** (.020)	.045 (.026)	.114** (.029)	.041 (.089)	.793** (.017)
27	-1.18 (6.2)	.082 (.067)	.035** (.012)	.009 (.025)	.015 (.014)	.089 (.072)	.958** (.013)
34	83.3** (26.4)	-.545** (.153)	.268** (.035)	.248** (.027)	.008 (.005)	.348* (.156)	.535** (.025)
35	54 (74)	.269 (.352)	.472** (.059)	.334** (.060)	.017* (.007)	.619 (.369)	.178** (.030)
36	27.4 (32)	.297 (.187)	.194** (.045)	.160** (.060)	.042** (.009)	-.575** (.204)	.528** (.031)

NOTE: Standard errors in parentheses.

SOURCE: Bureau of Census: Manufacturers' Shipments, Inventories, and Orders (1958-1976); monthly, nonadjusted.

*Indicates coefficients significant at the 5 percent level.

**Indicates coefficients significant at the 1 percent level.

This would be equivalent, in other words, to having zero values for the cross coefficients:

$$c_1 = c_3 = c_5 = d_2 = d_4 = d_6 = 0.$$

However, to the extent that goods produced by one process must "compete"[13] for factors of production with goods of the other process we could expect negative signs for the cross coefficients—*except* for c_3, the coefficient of H_{t-1}, where the presence of a larger stock of goods would enable *more* current production to order at the expense of production to stock.

Reflection for a moment on the decisions which the baker of chapter 4 would have to make, if there were a rush of new orders for cakes, is helpful. There would be "competition" for oven time, people time, raw materials, and shelf space. The baker would necessarily consider which products were of most immediate importance—in other words, scheduling decisions. Slightly longer range, he could consider possible adjustments in total output, such as hiring an

Table 12.   Estimated Coefficients for Industries with Unfilled Orders: Production to Stock. Quarterly Data, Seasonally Adjusted

Ind. No.	$P_t^S = d_0 + d_1 P_{t-1}^S + d_2 P_{t-1}^O + d_3 H_{t-1} + d_4 U_{t-1} + d_5 N_t^S + d_6 N_t^O$						
	d_0	d_1	d_2	d_3	d_4	d_5	d_6
26	-27.7**	.209*	.078**	-.292**	-.036	.848**	-.021
	(7.2)	(.097)	(.016)	(.043)	(.043)	(.099)	(.014)
27	26.1	-.052	.055	-.365**	-.105*	1.103**	-.004
	(16.6)	(.110)	(.030)	(.088)	(.041)	(.123)	(.027)
34	-21.4	.433**	-.014	-.093*	.012	.573**	.020
	(34.3)	(.107)	(.024)	(.037)	(.007)	(.107)	(.016)
35	25.3	.428**	.030*	-.131**	.005	.600**	-.002
	(32)	.101	(.014)	(.030)	(.004)	.108	(.007)
36	-37.6*	.351**	.070**	-.191**	-.010	.706**	-.013
	(17)	.097	(.019)	(.042)	(.006)	.103	(.010)

NOTE: Standard errors in parentheses.

SOURCE: Bureau of Census: Manufacturers' Shipments, Inventories, and Orders (1958-1976); quarterly, seasonally adjusted.

*Indicates coefficients significant at the 5 percent level.

**Indicates coefficients significant at the 1 percent level.

extra baker for evening work, etc. Note that the baker need not be up against an overall capacity restraint in order to find it necessary to revise schedules as demand changes, to make changes in working hours or number of employees, and so forth.

In the general case, it is fair to say that managers are *always* required to think (in profit-maximizing terms) which products are to be scheduled first (and on which lines), and how best to eke out additional production when business is brisk. Conversely, when business is slack,[14] they must allocate the smaller amount of production needed to the most appropriate facilities in cost-minimizing fashion. Or, to complete the earlier analogy, when business is slack, it is the production units which must "compete" for output.

Another cross effect is possible, which depends on the degree to which successive steps of manufacture *within* the industry are dependent on (or *induced* by) outputs of the same industry. For example, the manufacture of electric power cable (to order) in Industry 34 requires: (1) copper (or less frequently, aluminum) which originates from Industry 33, and (2) appropriate

Table 13. Estimated Coefficients for Industries with Unfilled Orders: Production to Stock. Quarterly Data, Nonadjusted

Ind. No.	$P_t^S = d_0 + d_1 P_{t-1}^S + d_2 P_{t-1}^O + d_3 H_{t-1} + d_4 U_{t-1} + d_5 N_t^S + d_6 N_t^O$						
	d_0	d_1	d_2	d_3	d_4	d_5	d_6
26	-27.7**	.209*	.078**	-.292**	-.036	.848**	-.021
	(7.2)	(.097)	(.016)	(.043)	(.043)	(.099)	(.014)
27	22.4	.357**	.091**	-.427**	-.112*	.702**	-.032*
	(22)	(.119)	(.015)	(.107)	(.054)	(.117)	(.016)
34	4.33	.125	-.025	-.109*	.028**	.865**	.015
	(53.9)	(.127)	(.032)	(.053)	(.010)	(.113)	(.019)
35	142.7*	.194	-.025	-.069	.022**	.784**	.003
	(55)	(.106)	(.018)	(.046)	(.006)	(.109)	(.009)
36	-59.8	.133	.133**	-.380**	-.012	.968**	-.032
	(41)	(.112)	(.030)	(.086)	(.012)	(.117)	(.019)

NOTE: Standard errors in parentheses.

SOURCE: Bureau of Census: Manufacturers' Shipments, Inventories, and Orders (1958-1976); quarterly, nonadjusted.

*Indicates coefficients significant at the 5 percent level.

**Indicates coefficients significant at the 1 percent level.

insulating and sheathing materials, say: PVC and polyethylene from Industry 28.

As indicated, in this case neither raw material is from Industry 34 so there are no induced effects within the industry. However, the copper must undergo two fabricating steps (to stock) in Industry 34: (1) smelting of copper ingot to copper rod, and (2) drawing of the copper rod into bare wire, before it can be insulated and cabled. Consequently, in *this* case, orders for, and production of, electric power cable cause *positive* cross effects by *inducing* orders for, and production of, copper rod and bare wire. It is true that they also induce orders/production for copper ingot (Industry 33) and polyethylene and PVC (Industry 28), but there are no cross effects here, because the impact of these orders is not felt in Industry 34.

The fabricated metals industry is particularly rich in examples of the type illustrated above.

Table 14.   Estimated Coefficients for Industries with Unfilled Orders: Production to Stock. Monthly Data, Seasonally Adjusted

Ind. No.	$P_t^S = d_0 + d_1 P_{t-1}^S + d_2 P_{t-1}^O + d_3 H_{t-1} + d_4 U_{t-1} + d_5 N_t^S + d_6 N_t^O$						
	d_0	d_1	d_2	d_3	d_4	d_5	d_6
26	-10.7**	.011	.175**	-.096**	-.020	1.051**	-.113**
	(2.87)	(.056)	(.021)	(.017)	(.018)	(.068)	(.016)
27	9.6	.144*	.066**	-.116**	-.035*	.903**	-.019
	(5.35)	(.064)	(.023)	(.026)	(.013)	(.081)	(.022)
34	2.0	.150*	-.045*	-.017	.007**	.836**	.031*
	(9.1)	(.066)	(.019)	(.010)	(.002)	(.065)	(.013)
35	23.5*	.027	.045**	-.055**	.004**	.997**	-.021*
	(10.7)	(.064)	(.015)	(.010)	(.001)	(.069)	(.008)
36	-14.7*	.079	.068**	-.061**	-.002	.971**	-.018
	(6.5)	(.059)	(.019)	(.016)	(.002)	(.066)	(.011)

NOTE: Standard errors in parentheses.

SOURCE: Bureau of Census: Manufacturers' Shipments, Inventories, and Orders (1958-1976); monthly, seasonally adjusted.

*Indicates coefficients significant at the 5 percent level.

**Indicates coefficients significant at the 1 percent level.

Production to Order: Own Effects

With this as preparation, we are ready to analytically review the test results presented on tables 8–15. To facilitate this part of our exercise, table 16 carries a summary of the signs and statistical significance of the parameter coefficients under examination. (Section C of the table summarizes the corresponding information from tables 2-5 for comparison).

To begin with the "own effects" coefficients of production to order: c_2, c_4, c_6, we observe that all coefficients are of the expected (+) sign. All c_6 and most c_2 are significant at the 1 percent level, but only one-third of the c_4's are significant even at 5 percent. The results are sensitive both to the length of the data period and to seasonal adjustment.

The two most important determinants of P_t^o, based on both size and significance of their coefficients, are sales expectations and the previous level of production. Together they account for the largest part of the P_t^o "decision."

Table 15.   Estimated Coefficients for Industries with Unfilled Orders: Production to Stock. Monthly Data, Nonadjusted

Ind. No.	$P_t^S = d_0 + d_1 P_{t-1}^S + d_2 P_{t-1}^O + d_3 H_{t-1} + d_4 U_{t-1} + d_5 N_t^S + d_6 N_t^O$						
	d_0	d_1	d_2	d_3	d_4	d_5	d_6
26	18.6	-.177	.249**	-.233*	-.301*	1.413**	-.013
	(23)	(.373)	(.091)	(.117)	(.129)	(.393)	(.077)
27	.183	.271**	.042**	-.028	-.002	.741**	-.030*
	(6.1)	(.069)	(.012)	(.025)	(.014)	(.071)	(.013)
34	7.8	.420**	-.034*	-.017	.007**	.564**	.018
	(10.1)	(.059)	(.014)	(.011)	(.002)	(.060)	(.010)
35	31	.378**	-.026**	-.010	.005**	.601**	.005
	(13)	(.060)	(.010)	(.010)	(.001)	(.068)	(.005)
36	-4.1	.378**	.000	-.048*	.007*	.626**	.004
	(11)	(.064)	(.015)	(.020)	(.003)	(.069)	(.011)

NOTE: Standard errors in parentheses.

SOURCE: Bureau of Census: Manufacturers' Shipments, Inventories, and Orders (1958-1976); monthly, nonadjusted.

*Indicates coefficients significant at the 5 percent level.

**Indicates coefficients significant at the 1 percent level.

However, the contribution of sales expectations is weightier in some industries than others. In Industry 27 the production pattern is heavily oriented toward new orders, while at the other extreme, for Industry 35, the previous rate of production (and the cost of changing production levels) is well the more significant contributor.

Unfilled orders, while positive as expected, appear to be a less important factor with the exception of the paper industry (Industry 26). For paper, the term is both larger and of greater significance than for the other industries.

Logically, this brings up a valid question—do differences, such as this last one, represent some form of failure of this type of model? After all, shouldn't all industries producing both to order and to stock follow the same pattern? The answer, which of necessity shall be developed in increments, is, "no." The underlying characteristics of the various industries differ, and it is one of the strengths of the present approach that differences in performance can be distinguished. There are, however, a certain number of signals which represent noise rather than substance; we plead merit, not infallibility.

With respect to the importance of unfilled orders for the paper industry, there are additional remarks later.

Production to Stock: Own Effects

The own effects coefficients for production to stock are d_1, d_3, and d_5 (from table 12–15). Almost all the expected signs, (+), (−), (+), respectively for the coefficients, are proper. The d_1 coefficient is incorrect (−) twice, once with the QS data and once with M. In each case it is the only result of those for the five industries which is not significant at least at the 5 percent level. We can conclude that overall the signs of the coefficients agree satisfactorily with what was expected of "proper" signs for production to stock.

The coefficient of sales expectations, d_5, is significant at the 1 percent level in all twenty observations; and the proportion of coefficients significant at the 5 percent level for d_1, and d_3 approximates that shown in tables 2–5 for the production to stock industries.

The next step is to inspect the pattern presented by the coefficients to see how well they resemble those of the industries first studied, i.e., those which produce only to stock; and also what differences exist between the "to stock" and "to order" functions of industries which produce in both ways. There are several qualitative comparisons which can be made, based on the size of the coefficients. First, two disclaimers are in order:

1. By qualitative comparisons, we mean a visual interpretation, and not a statistical test. We are looking at tendencies, not hard and fast boundaries.

2. One of the industries which accumulates unfilled orders, and hence is classed as producing both to stock and order is paper (Industry 26). However, as was first noticed when we looked at table 1, the pattern of the coefficients for Industry 26 resembled those of the industries producing to stock somewhat more than those of other industries producing both to stock and order.

The inference would be that the "to order" function is of comparatively less importance in Industry 26. Unfortunately, our models do not provide any information on the amount of proportion of production by each process. However, there is other information available. For instance, we could look at the ratio of unfilled orders to quarterly sales for each industry. A low figure for $\bar{U}_t / \bar{S}_t$ would suggest a lower dependence on sales to order, and a higher proportion of sales from stock. Listed below are the ratios of the mean values of unfilled orders, $\bar{U}_t$, to the mean value of quarterly sales, $\bar{S}_t$, over the 1958–1976 test period, for the five industries which accumulate unfilled orders.

Table 16. A Summary of the Signs and Significance of Parameter Coefficients for Industries Producing both to Stock and to Order

A. Production to Order Function: Industries 26, 27, 34, 35, 36

$$P_t^o = c_0 + c_1 P_{t-1}^S + c_2 P_{t-1}^o + d_3 H_{t-1} + d_4 U_{t-1} + d_5 N_t^S + d_6 N_t^o$$

	c_1			c_2 (own)			c_3			c_4 (own)			c_5			c_6 (own)		
	*	**	+	*	**	+	*	**	+	*	**	+	*	**	+	*	**	+
QS	2	1	0	4	5	4	2	2	4	1	1	5	1	1	5	5	5	5
Q	1	3	1	4	5	5	2	3	4	1	1	5	1	2	4	5	5	5
MS	1	1	1	3	5	5	3	3	5	1	2	5	2	1	2	5	5	5
M	3	1	3	5	5	5	3	3	5	2	3	5	4	3	4	5	5	5

NOTE: QS and Q mean quarterly data, respectively, seasonally adjusted and nonadjusted; MS and M mean monthly data, respectively, seasonally adjusted and nonadjusted.

+Signifies the number of industries with positive coefficients.

*Signifies the number of industries with coefficients significant at the 5 percent level.

**Signifies the number of industries with coefficients significant at the 1 percent level.

(continued)

TABLE 16 (continued)

B. Production to Stock Function: Industries 26, 27, 34, 35, 36

$$P_t^S = d_0 + d_1 P_{t-1}^S + d_2 P_{t-1}^O + d_3 H_{t-1} + d_4 U_{t-1} + d_5 N_t^S + d_6 N_t^O$$

	d₁ (own)			d₂			d₃ (own)			d₄			d₅ (own)			d₆		
	+	*	**	+	*	**	+	*	**	+	*	**	+	*	**	+	*	**
QS	4	4	3	4	3	2	5	5	4	2	4	0	5	5	5	1	*	0
Q	5	1	1	3	3	3	5	4	3	2	1	2	5	4	4	2	0	1
MS	5	2	0	4	5	4	5	4	4	2	3	2	5	5	5	1	1	3
M	4	4	4	3	4	3	5	2	0	3	4	2	5	5	5	3	0	1

C. Production to Stock (Only): Industries 20, 21, 28, 29

$$P_t = d_0 + d_1 P_{t-1} + d_2 H_{t-1} + d_3 N_t$$

	d₁			d₂			d₃		
	+	*	**	+	*	**	+	*	**
QS	3	1	1	0	3	3	4	4	4
Q	4	1	1	0	4	4	4	4	4
MS	3	2	1	0	4	4	4	4	4
M	3	3	3	0	3	3	4	4	4

Industry Number	$\bar{U}/\bar{S}_t$
26	.16
27	.04
34	1.18
35	1.54
36	1.33

For both Industries 26 and 27 it seems reasonable to conclude from the low ratio of unfilled orders to total sales, that while both stock and order processes are represented, their overall character probably more closely approximates the production to stock industries than is the case with Industries 34, 35, and 36.

Continuing with examination of table 16, sections B and C compare the characteristics of the production to stock of industries which also produce to order with industries producing to stock alone. Clearly, the most important parameter in each case is new orders, N_t, but with a generally lower range of values for the coefficients in section B.

The coefficients of H_{t-1} for Industries 34 and 35 are lower (and also, less significant) than the rest of the group, whose coefficients are quite similar in value and significance to those of section A. This suggests that the role of H_{t-1} as a parameter is about the same for the production to stock functions of Industries 26, 27, and 36 as is the case for industries producing only to stock— but, that H_{t-1} is a less important determinant for fabricated metals and machinery (Industries 34 and 35).

Finally, in comparing values of coefficients for P_{t-1}, it is evident for the production to stock function of industries which produce both to stock and order, that P_{t-1} is a determinant of greater importance in establishing a new level of production (i.e., implying higher costs involved in changing production levels) than is typically the case for industries producing only to stock. In fact, this tends to suggest that an important basic characteristic underlying whether industries tend to produce to both stock and order (instead of only to stock) is that the costs involved in changing production outputs tend to be higher for the former group. Alternatively, of course, this difference in range of value for the coefficients of P_{t-1} might simply indicate nonsupport of the premise under development, of the similarity in nature of processes producing to stock, whether or not accompanied by production to order. That the former conclusion appears supportable is reinforced by additional observations below.

Production to Order vs. Production to Stock

Using sections A and B together, we can make a comparison of the (own effects) coefficients for producing to stock and to order, within industries which do both.

The coefficients of N_t show new orders always to be an important determinant of the planned level of production to order, but not necessarily *the* most important. In fact, for production to order, it appears that the important factor is *a combination* of the new order parameter and the lagged production term—and, that as the latter becomes of greater importance, the former's weight declines inversely. For Industry 35, in fact, the "own" coefficient of P_{t-1}^o outweighs that of N_o^t. In other words, while important, the coefficient of N_t is not necessarily larger than that for P_{t-1} as is *always* the case for the production to stock function.

Or, to express the observation from the standpoint of the coefficient for P_{t-1}, the size and significance of the own coefficient shows a strong tendency to be larger for the production to order function, than for production to stock, for industries which produce in both ways. And, in turn, the coefficient for P_{t-1} is always larger than observed for industries which produce only to stock. This observation supports the earlier conclusion that the cost of changing the level of production in industries which produce both to order and to stock is a more significant factor than is the case for industries which produce to stock alone.

The coefficient for the U_{t-1} term is positive, as expected, for the production to order function. It is smaller, however, than that of the corresponding H_{t-1} term in the production to stock function. This is not surprising, for one would expect the (real) costs of carrying inventories to, in general, be more significant than the implied costs of carrying unfilled orders. That the results demonstrate this is, at least, intuitively, in the proper direction.

Qualitatively then, we could conclude:

1. The characteristics of the production to stock portions, of industries producing both to stock and order, are markedly similar to those of industries which produce only to stock.

2. Some of the industries which produce to both order and stock (e.g., Industries 34, 35, and 36) reflect greater costs for changes in production levels than is the case for the industries producing altogether (or mostly) to stock. This effect appears to carry over to the costs of changing production level for the *production to stock* segment of these same industries.

3. With the exception of Industry 27 (for which the reverse is true), the production to stock functions of industries which have both forms of production have *higher* coefficients accompanying the sales expectations term, and *lower* coefficients with the P_{t-1} term.

4. From the variations demonstrated in the various industries studied, it can be inferred that there are many differences in the underlying characteristics (e.g., cost, and financial) which account for them. These factors will be explored in succeeding chapters.

Cross Effects

The signs expected of "cross effects" coefficients depend on the nature of the predominant relations between the order and stock functions. These can be classed as:

Effects on Coefficient Signs

(a)	independent	0
(b)	"competing	$(-)$ [$(+)$ for the c_3 coefficient of H_1]
(c)	induced usage	$(+)$

Conclusions are less clear-cut for the cross effects. Significant coefficients are half as frequent, and there are a number of apparent reversals/inconsistencies.

The results are straightforward in some cases. For instance, production to order in the printing and publishing industry (Industry 27) appears *independent* of production to stock activities with c_1, c_3, c_5 coefficients ~ 0. In Industry 34, the cross coefficient, c_5, for new orders from stock is sizably positive and significant, as a determinant of the production to order function, implying that increases in production to order tend to accompany increased orders from stock (and hence production to stock)—an *induced* effect.

On the other hand, d_2, the cross coefficient of P_{t-1}^o for the production to stock function of Industry 35 is inconsistent. While it is significant three times out of four, the fact that it is negative with quarterly and monthly unadjusted data, and positive with quarterly and monthly seasonally adjusted data, probably has as much to say about collinearity and its effects on the estimated values of coefficients as it does about the real nature of this particular function.

One of the least ambiguous results was the positive sign for c_3, showing more production to order when inventories of stock products are up, in nearly every case. In most cases (and such qualifications are increasingly needed) there was a negative sign for c_1, indicating less production to order when the previous level of production to stock had been high—a *competitive* effect. The coefficient of new orders to stock, c_5, was largely positive for Industries 26, 34, 35, and 36 (interpreted as an *induced* effect); for Industry 27 it was essentially zero (*independent*).

The d_4 coefficient of U_{t-1} was significant and positive, though small, in Industries 34 and 35, indicative of an accumulation of unfilled orders *inducing* additional stock production. In Industries 26 and 27, and coefficients were negative in each case, signifying that the higher the backlog of unfilled orders, the more production to stock was limited (a *competitive* effect).

The d_6 coefficients of N_o^t for Industry 34 were all positive, though small, implying larger stock production *induced* by new orders to stock. The other

d_6's ranged from 0 to a scattering of negative numbers (some significant), the latter illustrative of a *competitive* effect in reduction of P_t^s.

Finally, d_2, the coefficient of P_{t-1}^o, was negative for all four data series for Industry 34, but generally positive and significant for the other industries. This would imply an *induced* effect (higher output to order calling for more production to stock).

Inventory Characteristics of the Different Industries

So far, references to "inventory" essentially have been to stocks of finished goods. These are, of course, only a part of total inventories. In this chapter, we will explore the characteristic manner in which various industries use/treat inventory as part of the manufacturing process.

First, definition of the three types of inventory:

1. Raw materials, RM, are those goods and products required as inputs for the manufacturing process. It was noted in chapter 5 that not infrequently the finished product of one firm is the raw material of another (e.g., copper rod → bare wire → electric power cable).

2. Work in progress, WIP, in the physical sense, represents partially finished products. More precisely, it is the total value of goods which have been started through the manufacturing process, but not yet completed (e.g., printed pages not yet bound). It implies multiple process steps.

3. With relatively minor exceptions, as earlier mentioned, inventories of finished goods, H_t, represent products ready for sale/delivery from processes which produce to stock.

Table 17 shows the proportion of total inventory represented by each of these three categories for the nine industries being examined. The figures are derived from quarterly data for the 1958–1976 period. The proportions are ratios of the means for each type of inventory over the period. Table 17 also shows mean values for total inventory, quarterly sales, and unfilled orders for the five industries which report them.

The most obvious points of table 17 are probably:

1. A proportionally huge RM holding in the tobacco industry.

2. Except for that observation, the inventories of industries producing to stock appear rather comparable. Finished goods represent about one-half

Table 17.   The Percentage of Inventories held as Raw Materials, Work-in-Process, and Finished Goods: Dollar Values of Total Inventories, Sales, and Unfilled Orders

Ind.	% RM	% WIP	% H_t	Inventories, INV $\$\overline{M}$	Sales $\overline{S}_t$, $\$\overline{M}$	Unfilled Orders $\overline{U}_t$, $\$\overline{M}$
20	35.5	7.5	57.1	8,328.1	24,286.5	–
21	91.6	1.5	6.9	2,384.6	1,333.6	–
28	38.1	15.1	46.8	5,855.6	11,960.7	–
29	24.5	21.8	53.7	2,318.1	7,345.1	–
26	53.4	10.8	35.9	2,519.8	6,076.8	949.9
27	40.9	24.1	34.9	2,024.9	5,899.2	505.9
34	38.7	34.1	27.2	7,186.9	10,493.2	12,408.9
35	26.9	44.3	28.8	11,985.9	13,226.4	20,377.2
36	27.9	46.1	26.0	7,918.3	10,567.0	14,088.6

[a]Percentages are mean values, 1958-1976, of the proportion each inventory category represents of total inventory.

[b]Dollar figure (in millions of dollars) means for 1958-1976, from quarterly non-adjusted BuCensus data

of total inventory for three industries, and WIP is clearly the smallest category in each case.

3. Inventories for industries producing both to stock and order show larger proportions held of either (or both) RM and WIP than finished goods. This is particularly the case for the three durable goods industries.

4. For the latter three industries, the overall size of inventories in relation to sales appears much larger. Examination of this point is easier, using table 18, which shows the ratio of inventory, by type, to quarterly sales, and also finished goods inventories and unfilled orders expressed in days.

As has been done in table 18, it is convenient to express inventory data from different industries as ratios or proportions of sales, to put the figures on a common basis. Another ratio frequently encountered is expressed as *days*—i.e., the ratio of the size of a given stock to *average sales per day*.[1]

And, it appears that we have an inventory of points for discussion.

Table 18.   Raw Materials, Work-in-Process, and Finished Goods
Inventories, and Total Inventory Expressed as a Ratio of Sales: Finished
Goods Inventory and Unfilled Orders Expressed in Days of Sales

Ind.	RM/S_t	WIP/S_t	H_t/S_t	INV/S_t	H_t, Days	U_t Days
20	.1223	.02526	.1988	.3464	17.9	–
	(.00954)	(.00246)	(.01404)			
21	1.682	.0255	.11634	1.824	10.5	–
	(.2645)	(.00764)	(.04723)			
28	.1824	.0724	.2339	.4887	21.1	–
	(.0172)	(.0058)	(.0237)			
29	.07985	.0757	.1961	.3517	17.7	–
	(.00821)	(.0137)	(.0454)			
26	.2232	.0468	.1474	.4174	13.3	14.1
	(.0187)	(.00575)	(.0117)			
27	.1422	.0020	.1187	.3435	10.7	7.7
	(.01242)	(.0068)	(.0129)			
34	.2706	.2351	.1833	.6890	16.5	106.4
	(.0310)	(.0151)	(.0241)			
35	.2376	.4002	.2638	.9016	23.7	138.6
	(.0266)	(.0298)	(.0265)			
36	.2036	.3372	.1953	.7361	17.6	120.0
	(.0241)	(.0362)	(.0174)			

[a] Standard deviations are in parentheses.

[b] H_t (in days) $= \dfrac{H_t}{\text{av. daily sales}} = \dfrac{H_t}{S_t/90}$ (since S_t represents a 90-day sales figure).

[c] U_t (in days) is derived similarly.

Raw Materials

Amounts held in raw material inventory (RM), represent what is needed as
input for immediately forthcoming production *plus* whatever cushion
prudence dictates (on a cost minimizing basis) to protect against the cost of
interruptions to manufacture (or, on occasion, to hedge against anticipated
price changes). The pattern of the tobacco industry, Industry 21, clearly goes
beyond this. Its behavior is explained as an attempt to insure consistent quality

of end product (by blending and aging) from an inherently variable raw material.[2]

How large should the inventory of a raw material be?

The answer is readily calculable in a simple case, e.g., a one input process, such as use of ortho-xylene by a chemical firm, to make phthalic anhydride. The ortho-xylene is delivered in tank cars (which provides the unit increment). The process runs at a design-established rate which provides the daily requirement. There are also: average and maximum transit times for rail delivery from suppliers; the quantity on order but not yet delivered (which, added to that on hand, gives the amount *on view*); costs of down time were there no 0-x on hand; and cost of funds tied up for any given size inventory.

However, for products requiring hundreds, or even thousands of different parts and materials (many of which may be used in several or many other products) the processes both of calculation and control are appreciably more difficult. Since running out of *any one* component can delay completion,[3] or halt the multi-product process, the statistical inference is that larger cushions are needed in the multi-component case. In addition, the *costs* of monitoring the RM inventory tend to rise exponentially, as the number of materials increases.

Obviously, overstocking materials used in low volume represents less of an increase in holding costs than the overstocking of large runners. Various approaches have been devised in the past, along the "ABC" approach of dividing RM components into three groups based on activity. Loosely following a normal distribution, the first 12 percent numerically of items stocked might be expected to represent 56 percent of the total cost of requirements. The next 42 percent of the items would account for 38 percent more of total cost; and the final 46 percent of the stock for only 6 percent of total cost. By concentrating on the "A" items of the large volume group, giving routine attention to the B's, and only perfunctory attention to the C's, costs of control could be at least halved.

A commonly encountered system of minimal attention for small volume items was known as the "two bin" system. Two storage bins worth were ordered to start. When one was exhausted, use of the second began, and an order was put in to replace the contents of the first bin.

The computer now provides a low cost approach to handling the large amounts of information inherent in manufacturing processes utilizing multiple parts and components. The approach is known as material requirements planning, MRP, and it is concerned with maximum efficient in timing of orders for RM, minimizing investment in on-hand inventory, and at the same time providing assurance of needed stocks for planned production runs.[4] MRP may be expected to provide benefits both in inventory reduction, and in costs of order-handling and scheduling. Industries with proportionally large RM inventories, and with processes utilizing multiple components, such as Industries 34, 35, and 36, in this study should be particularly benefitted.

The relatively high RM of the paper industry, Industry 26, also deserves comment. It represents a bulky raw material (logs) purchased on site, which require collection and transportation. This is simply an industry characteristic. MRP does not apply.

Work-in-Process

Another distinguishing feature of the characteristics of Industries 34, 35, 36, and to a lesser extent Industry 27 is the relatively high work-in-process, or WIP inventory. It is indicative of the types of manufacturing process encountered in these industries.

Work-in-process is inherently a rather mixed bag. It can represent, for example, whiskey aging in the keg. However, at least for Industries 34, 35, and 36 which show particular reliance upon it, it tends to reflect sub-assemblies and semi-finished goods, which must pass through a series of machine steps before completion. Process, or "lead" time for manufacture of these products involves a series of "set-up times," "running times," etc., but typically 90 percent of the time is not process time per se, but queue or waiting time for the next step.

> Therefore, a large proportion of the dollars invested in work in process inventory is tied up in nonproductive idle goods. This indicates that the major paybacks in reducing work in process inventories may be gained through reduction of queues rather than process, set-up, or run times.[5]

The authors of this quotation also believe that MRP is a logical part of the control of WIP inventory, as well as its RM function.

If the MRP proponents are correct in their assertions, we could expect in coming years to see an even sharper reduction in WIP within the Industries 34, 35, and 36 areas than will be accomplished in RM control.

In the case both of RM and WIP inventories, the point has been made that it is the characteristics of the manufacturing processes of the industry which determine inventory levels and characteristics—rather than the reverse.

Finished Goods and Unfilled Orders

The considerable dependence on sizable RM and WIP inventories of industries producing both to stock and order (particularly, Industries 34, 35, and 36) has been commented upon. It brings up a question, however, "If the manufacturing characteristics of industries producing to both stock and order differ so much from the industries producing only to stock, *why* are the ratios of H_t/S_t (or H_t in days) so much alike for the two groups?"

The answer is that the differences are camouflaged. To start with, total sales of Industries 26, 27, 34, 35, and 36 (or of the sales per day equivalent figure when the answer is expressed in days) has not been properly used as the denominator for H_t and U_t. Since H_t is held for sales from stock, S_t^s, and U_t are accumulated for sales to order, S_t^o, the proper denominators to express H_t and U_t in "days of sales" would be S_t^s and S_t^o respectively.

We know, of course, that total sales, $S_t = S_t^s + S_t^o$ but information about the values of the latter terms is not available. What *is* apparent, is that both S_t^s and S_t^o must be smaller than S_t, which was used in the preparation of table 18, so properly estimated, the various ratios would all be larger. For example, if sales were evenly split between order and stock for Industry 34, H_t in days would be increased to 33 days while U_t would be 213 days.

Let us pause for a moment to consider what additional clues we have been given about the natures of Industries 34, 35, and 36:

1. The d_1 and c_2 "own effects" coefficients of P_{t-1}^s and P_{t-1}^o in chapter 5 were large and significant. Costs of changing production levels are therefore indicated to be significant decision factors in these industries. At the same time, the production to order "decision" was only slightly responsive to the level of unfilled orders. Together, the inference is that changes in production levels in these industries are relatively cumbersome/expensive.
2. The RM levels held in Industries 34, 35, and 36 are roughly twice as large (in proportion to sales) as those in Industries 20, 28, and 29, which produce to stock. This would tend to indicate (though it does not *prove*) that the manufacturing processes of the first group require very large numbers of component parts. (However, large raw materials inventories can also reflect special problems such as those of the paper and tobacco industries, noted earlier.)
3. The very large work-in-process inventories (as a proportion of sales) are a more positive clue. For example, in Industry 36, if we were to estimate the value of "typical" work-in-process as representing perhaps 75 percent[6] of its ultimate contribution to finished product value, and using S_t in the denominator for want of having the unknown (but smaller) S_t^o, then WIP would represent at least a forty days' stock. And, since some of the "jobs" will have been in process longer than others, we have an indication that the typical "dwell time" of work-in-process would be of the order of magnitude of at least eighty days.
4. Finally, U_t, expressed in days, for Industry 36 is 120 days, or longer, depending on the actual size of S_t^o. Since this is a longer period than the eighty days guesstimated in (3), we could infer that work does not begin for manufacture to order as quickly as orders are received, but that there is usually an initial waiting period.

Fitting all these pieces together, a pattern is portrayed of multi-step, multi-component manufacturing for our durable goods industries, with built-in lags and delays, and with significant expenses incurred for changes in the rate of production. We will leave it to observers familiar with these industries to judge how accurate the portrait. We have carried the information built into the model a creditable distance. The limited objective of this portion of the study is showing that the information which has been developed is useful and usable in characterization of industry (or, ultimately, firm) performance, rather than attempting completely to characterize performance, per se. The argument, in other words, is meant to develop the idea of what are the importance and role of decision factors facing the profit-maximizing firm. The girth of this study, within these limits, is sufficient illustration of the need for limits to be placed.

It was an original intention of the study at this point to use a comparison of coefficients of the production functions studied, plus inspection of the inventory and unfilled order data, to infer the approximate size of the production to stock process in each of the five industries producing both to stock and order. Some plausible conclusions are possible, depending on assumptions, of course. The problem is that different assumptions result in different conclusions, and unfortunately no basis for testing the results is available. Hence, except for the qualitative thought that Industries 34, 35, and 36 appear to produce predominantly to order, and Industries 26 and 27 to stock, we have no more points immediately to pursue for the industries producing both to stock and order.

However, there are some interesting points relating to the industries producing only to stock which lend themselves to closer evaluation.

Production to Stock

We start by seeing how well inventory statistics for the nineteen year test period (1958–1976) correlate with the quarterly production of each of the four industries producing to stock.[7] For this purpose, the correlation matrices are shown in table 19.

With the usual exception of Industry 21, the correlations of the various categories of inventory with each other and with P_t are good. Even Industry 21's figures appear "reasonable," once one looks beyond the rather unusual raw material category.

However, as the standard deviations of the mean ratios of inventory components to sales (shown in table 18) demonstrated, there have been some substantial variations from the means. For instance, the mean of the ratio of finished goods to sales, $(\overline{H_t/S_t})$ for the tobacco industry (Industry 21), has a mean value of .11634 but the rather large standard deviation of .04723. We would expect, therefore, that 95 percent of the values would lie within the two sigma range .0219–.2108. Or out of a population of seventy-six samples,

Table 19.   Correlation Matrices for Production, Raw Materials, Work-in-Process, and Finished Goods for Production to Stock Industries: Quarterly Data, 1958-1976

	P_t	RM	WIP	H_t	P_t	RM	WIP	H_t
	Industry 20				Industry 21			
P_t	1.000	.971	.965	.982	1.000	.689	.782	.885
RM		1.000	.938	.960		1.000	.682	.678
WIP			1.000	.941			1.000	.814
H_t				1.000				1.000
	Industry 28				Industry 29			
P_t	1.000	.983	.987	.965	1.000	.987	.986	.975
RM		1.000	.992	.955		1.000	.986	.964
WIP			1.000	.978			1.000	.967
H_t				1.000				1.000

NOTE: P_t = production (quarterly); RM = raw materials inventory, end of quarter; WIP = work-in-process inventory, end of quarter; H_t = finished goods inventory, end of quarter.

perhaps four might be *outside* the range. Sure enough, there are four observations, listed below, all of which are out of the range on the high side:

Quarter	(H_t/S_t)
1974-1	.2551
1974-2	.2226
1976-2	.2112
1976-3	.2128

Now, on the face of it, this performance is not consistent with the idea frequently expressed of H_t/S_t being a relatively constant ratio. A detailed look at the data would seem in order. Table 20 shows data for each quarter from 1963-01 through the fourth quarter of 1976.[8] The fourth column shows the percentage ratio of H_t/S_t for each quarter.

As one's eye runs down the column showing H_t, the finished goods inventory at the end of the quarter, there is an interesting progression: (1)

through 1968, a regular seasonal pattern of inventory build-up in the first and second quarters, and depletion in the third and fourth; (2) next, a rather tentative four-year period which shows net inventory depletion in 1969 and 1970, and a restoral to the earlier level in 1971 and 1972; (3) beginning with 1972-04 there is a large build-up of H_t over the six quarter period till 1974-01, and (4) a stable period, thereafter.

If we compare the statistics for periods (1) plus (2) with (4) (ignoring the transitional build-up of (3)), we have:

Period	$\overline{H_t/S_t}$	Standard Deviation	2 Sigma Range
1963–1972	.0913	.0149	.0615–.1211
1974-03-1976	.1941	.0164	.1613–.2267

Some useful observations can be drawn from this exercise:

1. During 1958–1976, the tobacco industry changed its finished goods inventory pattern from typically holding eight days ($H/S = .0913$) to a seventeen day holding. The change in level makes for a large standard deviation in the ratio of finished goods to sales over the period as a whole, but actually, each of the periods shows relatively nonvariable behavior.

   In fact, a large part of the modest variability shown up through 1972 was regular and seasonal in nature—and seasonal variations will be investigated in the next chapter.

2. The shift from one inventory policy to another can be taken to reflect some basic structural changes in the market demand for tobacco products, and/or their pricing. And, in fact, no other industry has the distinction of a product sold bearing a Warning from the Surgeon-General!

In addition, cigarette smokers will recall the approximately fourfold increase in the price of their habit which occurred through the 1970s. While dollar volume of product did not decrease, because of this, quite obviously *physical volume* of sales did. It is logical, of course, from the buffer stock motive for holding finished goods, to expect that a smaller volume of physical goods sold would be accompanied by manufacturers holding a larger ratio of finished goods in proportion to sales.

Petroleum Industry

Changes in the pattern of inventory holdings occur for other reasons, too. The petroleum industry (Industry 29), through the entire test period (1958–1976) has faced a predictable, and predictably growing, demand. Yet, table 18 gives a

Table 20. Quarterly Sales, Production, and Finished Goods of the
Tobacco Industry (1963-1976), in Millions of Dollars, and the Quarterly
Ratio of Finished Goods to Sales

Quarter	S_t	P_t	H_t	H_t/S_t
1963-01	1,063	1,080	131	12.3
1963-02	1,160	1,169	140	12.1
1963-03	1,158	1,149	131	11.3
1963-04	1,141	1,118	108	9.5
1964-01	1,024	1,030	114	11.1
1964-02	1,197	1,207	124	10.4
1964-03	1,227	1,213	110	9.0
1964-04	1,205	1,191	96	8.0
1965-01	1,130	1,158	124	11.0
1965-02	1,193	1,201	132	11.0
1965-03	1,185	1,171	118	10.1
1965-04	1,141	1,119	96	8.4
1966-01	1,146	1,168	118	10.3
1966-02	1,206	1,219	131	10.9
1966-03	1,232	1,220	119	9.7
1966-04	1,188	1,164	95	8.1
1967-01	1,133	1,141	103	9.1
1967-02	1,254	1,263	112	8.9
1967-03	1,285	1,282	109	8.5
1967-04	1,231	1,222	100	8.1

(continued)

TABLE 20 (continued)

Quarter	S_t	P_t	H_t	H_t/S_t
1968-01	1,171	1,183	112	10.1
1968-02	1,251	1,262	123	9.8
1968-03	1,276	1,267	114	8.9
1968-04	1,239	1,237	112	9.0
1969-01	1,162	1,180	130	11.2
1969-02	1,284	1,277	123	10.1
1969-03	1,306	1,290	107	8.2
1969-04	1,240	1,241	108	8.7
1970-01	1,219	1,197	86	7.1
1970-02	1,324	1,324	86	7.0
1970-03	1,404	1,404	86	6.1
1970-04	1,403	1,412	95	7.0
1971-01	1,305	1,323	113	9.0
1971-02	1,401	1,398	110	8.0
1971-03	1,438	1,436	108	7.5
1971-04	1,384	1,385	109	8.0
1972-01	1,401	1,412	120	9.0
1972-02	1,475	1,480	125	9.0
1972-03	1,518	1,517	124	8.2
1972-04	1,525	1,542	141	9.3
1973-01	1,473	1,527	195	13.2
1973-02	1,599	1,643	239	14.9
1973-03	1,627	1,661	273	17.0

(continued)

TABLE 20 (continued)

Quarter	S_t	P_t	H_t	$H_t S_t$
1973-04	1,642	1,711	342	21.0
1974-01	1,631	1,705	416	26.0
1974-02	1,770	1,748	394	22.3
1974-03	1,861	1,828	361	19.4
1974-04	1,877	1,860	344	18.3
1975-01	1,835	1,867	376	21.0
1975-02	1,910	1,887	353	19.0
1975-03	1,945	1,941	349	18.0
1975-04	2,115	2,110	344	16.3
1976-01	1,975	2,023	392	19.8
1976-02	1,979	2,005	418	21.1
1976-03	1,978	1,981	421	21.3
1976-04	2,154	2,184	451	20.9

NOTE: S_t = quarterly sales, $\$\overline{M}$; P_t = quarterly produc-
tion, $\$\overline{M}$; H_t = quarter ending finished goods inventory, $\$\overline{M}$;
H_t/S_t = ratio of finished goods to sales, %.

mean value for (H_t/S_t) of .1961, and a standard deviation of .0454, which
means a two-sigma range of .1053–.2869. Can the sales of an industry of
predictable demand vary sufficiently to account for swings of this magnitude?

The behavior of the industry will be examined, this time with the use of
monthly data, so our first step is to note that monthly data over the same period
yield the following statistics:

		For April Only
$[\overline{H_t S_t}]_m =$	.583	.567
Standard deviation =	.141	.154
Two sigma range =	.301–.866	.259–.875

Data for the month of April for the period 1958–1977 are shown in table
21. The fourth column gives the ratio of $H_t S_t$, which (fairly) steadily declines
from ~ .74 to ~ .27, which is in keeping with two sigma range shown above.

Table 21.   Monthly Sales, Finished Goods, and the Ratio of Finished
Goods to Sales for the Petroleum Industry (1958-1977, for the April
Months only), in Millions of Dollars

Year	S_t	H_t	H_t/S_t	$0.01 \times H_t/\sqrt{S_t}$
1958	1,200	889	.741	.2566
1959	1,320	889	.673	.2447
1960	1,402	900	.642	.2404
1961	1,370	1,016	.742	.2745
1962	1,383	962	.696	.2587
1963	1,472	1,051	.714	.2739
1964	1,500	1,078	.719	.2783
1965	1,553	1,071	.690	.2718
1966	1,710	1,046	.612	.2529
1967	1,812	1,110	.607	.2584
1968	1,863	1,142	.613	.2646
1969	1,974	1,111	.563	.2501
1970	2,024	1,209	.597	.2687
1971	2,224	1,212	.545	.2570
1972	2,399	1,201	.501	.2452
1973	2,595	1,151	.444	.2259
1974	4,652	1,526	.328	.2237
1975	5,312	1,937	.365	.2658
1976	6,645	1,855	.279	.2276
1977	7,597	2,031	.267	.2330

The fifth column is a tabulation of H_t divided by *the square root* of S_t, times a constant, with the size of the constant chosen to yield figures of the same order of magnitude as those in column 4. The statistics listed below summarize the information of the fourth and fifth columns:

	H_t/S_t	$0.01 \times H_t/\sqrt{S_t}$
Mean	.567	.2536
Standard deviation	.1542	.0169
Two sigma range	.259–.875	.2197–.2875

The results in the fifth column appear to be a good illustration of Whitin's maxim that the profit-maximizing firm should increase its buffer inventories of finished goods, H_t, as the square root of S_t, rather than proportionally with S_t.[9]

Logically, a similar rationale should apply to the raw materials inventories of Industry 29. A test of this does, in fact, yield a relatively stable value,

$$\frac{RM}{\sqrt{S_t}} \sim 11.0$$

from 1958 through 1970. From 1971 on, however, the $RM/\sqrt{S_t}$ ratio increases in value. It is possible that the square root rule would work better for the entire period if the *physical volume* of the crude oil held by refineries was examined, instead of the dollar value as in this test (for it is in the period from 1971 on that oil prices have most rapidly risen). Such a test has not been made here, however.

A pause for a moment is in order, to recapitulate. In much of the literature dealing with inventories, the desired ratio of inventory to sales has been treated as a more or less set figure about which actually observed results tend to fluctuate (as governed by various formulations incorporating flexible and variable accelerators). However, the two examples investigated in recent pages have served to demonstrate that a relatively large shift may be made in the ratio (e.g., in response to change in demand), or progressively (e.g., as in following a Whitin-type square root approach for profit-maximization).

Other factors may also play a part, including financial ones, as the next example may help to explore.

There is also the point to be made, or more properly the *reminder,* that it is not the "behavior" of inventory which is being examined, but rather the manner in which firms (and, by extension, industries) handle their inventories.

Chemical Industry

The chemical industry, Industry 28, was reported, in table 18, as having a mean ratio for H_t/S_t of .2339 over the 1958–1976 period, and a standard deviation of .0237. The question to be examined is, "Is that more or less constant—or is that variable behavior?"

A quick overall impression from a graph is often helpful. Figure 4 shows two functions: (1) the (quarterly) H_t/S_t ratio, whose statistics were noted above; (2) the percent increase (decrease) in sales of the industry from the quarter before. The inclusion of the latter function will assist interpretation.

A number of observations can be made from figure 4:

1. Third and fourth quarter sales generally decrease, or show only a small increase. On the other hand, the largest sales increases each year are fairly regular in the first quarter, with the next largest increase in the second quarter.

2. Using the ΔS line as a visual aid, one can discern a fairly regular pattern of the final goods inventory being run down during the high second quarter sales, and of increasing inventory at year end (in anticipation of first quarter sales increases).

   Seasonal effects of this sort are further investigated in the next chapter.

3. Over the first eleven years (1958–1968-04), the H_t/S_t ratio is fairly flat (except for the seasonal wiggles).

4. This was followed by a steep two year climb to a peak value for H_t/S_t of .2954 in the fourth quarter of 1970. From there until the second quarter of 1974 there is a stepwise, but fairly linear decline to a minimum of .1666, or an H_t/S_t ratio only 56 percent of the preceding peak.

5. Finally, from 1974-04 on, for H_t/S_t there is another flat period, at a somewhat lower level than the first.

   The statistics for the four periods are:

Period	Quarters Included	$[\overline{H_t/S_t}]$	SD	Number of Observations (n)
I	1958-01–1968-04	.23547	.01677	44
II	1969-01–1970-03	.25538	.01323	7
III	1970-04–1974-03	.23146	.03899	16
IV	1974-04–1976-04	.21743	.01232	9

(SD is the abbreviation for standard deviation).

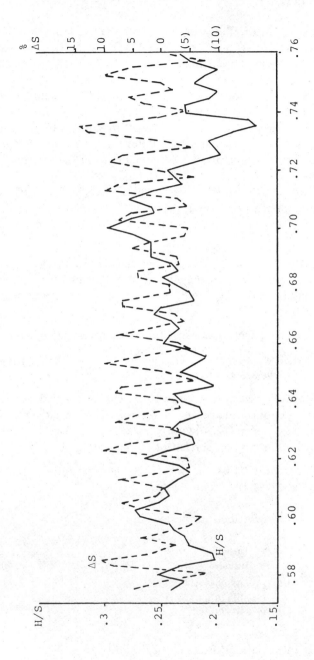

Figure 4. Industry 28 (1958-1976). Quarterly Percent
Change in Sales, and H/S Ratio

We will test the differences between the sample mean, $\bar{X}_I$, of the first period, and the means of the latter three periods to see if we can distinguish a difference (i.e., do the succeeding periods actually represent different populations, or are they simply continuations of the initial period)? Our null hypothesis, then, is:

$$H_o: (\mu_I - \mu_t) = 0$$

and the alternate hypothesis is simply that the means are not equal. We can use a two-tailed test[10] of the small-sample confidence interval between the means $(\mu_I - \mu_t)$, where μ_t represents the mean being tested of periods II–IV. The test statistic is:

$$t = \frac{X_I - X_t}{\sqrt{S_p^2 \left(\dfrac{1}{44} + \dfrac{1}{n_t}\right)}}$$

and

$$S_p^2 = \frac{(44-1) \cdot (.01677)^2 + (n_t-1) \cdot (S_t^2)}{44 - n_t - 2}$$

The test results:

t	Periods
-2.988	I:II
.5599	I:III
3.035	I:IV

And we can reject the null hypothesis (at the 1 percent level) for periods II and IV; but with this test we cannot reject it for period III. However, there is another tack available, based on the earlier observation that in period III, H_t/S_t declined in fairly linear fashion. And, in fact, if we apply an OLSQ regression to the period III observations, the relation is derived:

$$[H/S]_i = .29434 - .00786 \cdot (i - 1)$$

where $i = 1, 2, \ldots 16$ respectively for each of the sixteen observations of period III. The standard deviation of the regression is .0121 (assuming a normal distribution more or less about the trend line).

Adoption of the assumption that a linear relation is a good representation of distribution of the period III data is tantamount to accepting that its sixteen samples were not drawn from the same population as period I, because a normal distribution has been assumed for the latter. Further demonstration that this conclusion is reasonable can be based on the following points:

1. The two-sigma range for variation about the mean H_t/S_t of period I is .20193–.26901. We would expect 95 percent of samples drawn from a population like period I's to fall within this range.

2. However, of the sixteen observations of period III, there are eight altogether outside these limits (three on the high side, and five on the low).

3. It is reasonable to conclude that if eight of sixteen samples from the period III population lie outside the two-sigma range of period I, that *indeed, the populations are different*—even though, as we saw at the beginning, the means of the two periods are rather close.

Having reached the conclusion that the chemical industry has made changes, between 1958 and 1976, in its proportional holdings of finished goods inventories, we have the question to explore—why? An obvious starting point for changes in the behavior of profit-maximizing firms would, of course, be their profits.

1. To begin a step back, industry sales revenues had grown more or less steadily from 1958 through 1968-IQ at roughly a 5.5 percent rate. Then, from 1968-2Q through 1970, quarterly sales were essentially flat:

1968-2Q	$11,542 $\bar{M}$
1970-4Q	$11,576 $\bar{M}$

    This did not, as one might think, reflect a limitation on the availability of production capacity. The NBER IPXN 28 series for the period shows industry capacity to have been utilized only at about the rate of 83 percent.

2. The industry's before tax profit margins, defined as:

    $$\frac{\$ \text{ Earnings before Tax}}{\$ \text{ Sales}}$$

    had been essentially level from 1958 through 1965. They then began to slide lower reaching a (for then) low of 9.4 percent at the beginning of 1970. There was a modest recovery in profit margins for a few years, with another, even lower point reached at the end of 1974. A summary of this (plus accompanying data on short-term borrowings of the industry, and the interest rates on commercial loans from banks) is shown in table 22.

Table 22.   Profit Margins of the Chemical Industry, Short-Term Debt,
and Interest Rate (1958-1976), Quarterly

Period	Profit Margin, %	SD, %	Short-Term Debt Ratio, %	SD, %	Interest Rate, %
1958-1-1965-4	13.8	.9	4.2	.8	∿ 5
1966-1-1969-2	12.7	.8	8.6	1.5	5.5 increasing to 7.9
1969-3-1970-4	11.2	.5	11.5	.8	8.1-8.9
1970-1	9.4		12.0		8.5
1970-4-1974-3	11.6	1.1	11.0	1.3	initially 6.5, down to 5.5, then increasing to 12.4
1974-4	8.8		11.4		12.4
1974-4-1976-4	10.8	1.2	10.4	2.3	initially 12.4, decreasing to 7.3

[a]Profit margin = $\dfrac{\text{\$ Earnings before Tax}}{\text{Sales}}$.

[b]Short-term debt ratio = $\dfrac{\text{Short-term Debt}}{\text{Sales}}$.

[c]Interest rates = interest rates (annual %) on short-term business loans.

SOURCE: [a,b]FTC Quarterly Reports, Industry 28; [c]NBER, FY35R Series.

The latter components have been included in table 22, because it would be logical to assume a degree of working capital stricture resulting from the profit margin erosion and consequent poorer cash flow. And, in fact, chemical firms began to have increasing recourse to short-term loans. Through 1968, the highest debt/sales ratio utilized by the chemical industry had been 6.8 percent (in 1966-1). Suddenly, in 1967, the ratio jumped to 10.2 percent, and by 1971-1 it was up to 13.1 percent. Fairly steady declines in the debt ratio ensued through 1974. In 1975-1, probably reflecting financing needs from an abrupt short-term increase in inventories, the loan ratio reached a record high of 15.2 percent. Except for this aberration, the loan ratio declined fairly steadily to 8.1 percent by the end of 1976.

Quite obviously, the changes recited above in short-term borrowing practices of chemical firms reflected significant departures from previous norms.

Loans, of course, have an interest cost. The NBER FY 35R series for the cost of short-term business loans shows:

Period	% Interest
1958–1965-3	~ 5%
1965-4–1967	~ 6%
1968	6.7%
And then, the money crunch of late 1969, early 1970:	8.85%
1970	~ 8.5%

Though even higher interest rates have been more recently encountered, 8 1/2–9 percent was then *an astronomical* figure. But even overriding the interest rate was the danger that a firm could not get credit (or sufficient credit)—hence the term CRUNCH.

At this point, we turn to another factor—costs. "Contrary to theoretical expectations, most statistical cost function studies show that 'marginal cost is constant'"[11]—at least over the relevant range of output.

Consider a chemical firm operating at less than 85 percent capacity. Typically, capital investment is large, fixed costs high; and in ranges well short of capacity it is almost axiomatic in the industry that to lower the perceived "actual" cost (i.e., average cost) it is necessary to take advantage of essentially constant incremental costs (i.e., flat MC) and to increase output. Vice versa, a reduction in output "increases cost." This, of course, sets the stage for the firm to make a classic, but oft-repeated (in business annals) error.

1. To keep costs down, during the year plus period from 1968-2 through 1970-4, *in the face of flat or declining sales,* chemical manufacturers were reluctant to reduce production rates. Inescapably, this meant growth of inventories of finished goods—note the overall increase in H_t listed below, averaging $70 $\bar{M}$ per quarter.

2. The shrinkage of cash flow from lower profit margins meant increased use of short-term borrowing to "finance" the expanded finished goods inventories. The alternative, of course, of not increasing inventories would have called for lower production rates, hence lower profits and cash flows—of itself, an unfavorable factor in terms of its effect on needs for short-term credit.

What did firms actually do during this period? They relied apparently on a strategy more appropriate to ecclesiastical matters than to this particular business period—the doctrine of "speremos melitur" was followed. Alas, things became worse, not better:

Quarter	S_t, $\bar{M}$	P_t, $\bar{M}$	DH, $\bar{M}$
1968-1	10,718	10,832	114
2	11,542	11,421	(121)
3	11,369	11,357	(12)
4	11,222	11,344	122
1969-1	11,714	11,964	250
2	12,244	12,208	(36)
3	11,877	11,854	(23)
4	11,588	11,746	158
1970-1	12,276	12,463	187
2	12,257	12,631	74
3	12,098	12,124	26
4	11,578	11,679	103

As interest rates began to approximate mean profit margins (which by very slight extension implies exceeding those of weaker competitors') firms found themselves unable to afford the credit they needed. Which points up the most troublesome aspect of a credit crunch period. Which is worse—not being able to afford the borrowing of needed funds, or *not being able* to borrow them?

We postulate that this 1970 experience explains the steep decline for the next three and a half years in the industry's H/S ratio—no manager was *ever again* going to be caught in a credit crunch with his inventories high.

A simple regression test was performed, of the interplay between the factors examined above, over the four periods of varying H_t/S_t behavior which were identified at the beginning of this section. The model used was:

$$\frac{SHLN}{S_t} = a \cdot \frac{H_t}{S_t} + b \cdot \frac{Prof}{S_t} + c \cdot i + e_t. \qquad (6.1)$$

The model is hardly complete,[12] nor is it based on a theoretical foundation which would make it useful in predition of future short-term borrowing behavior. Its purpose is simply to provide an initial indication of the interplay between the factors treated. The results, presented in table 23, while not robust, are interesting.

$\bar{R}^2$'s are modest, but in a reasonable range. The Durbin-Watson test statistics tend to indicate an incidence of serial correlation. One specific difficulty encountered, of course, is the effects of the relative shortness of period II (1969-1–1970-3) and period IV (1974-4–1976-4) re the significance of the coefficients for each.

For the entire 1958-1976 test period, the coefficients are reported as significant at the 1 percent level. The positive value of "a" is indicative that a higher (finished goods) inventory ratio induces more borrowing. The negative "b" supports the expectation expressed earlier that more dependence on short-term debt can be expected when profit margins are lower. A negative

Table 23. Regression Results for an Initial Financial Test: Short-Term Debt of the Chemical Industry as a Function of Inventory to Sales Ratio, Profit Margins and Interest Rates (1958-1976), Quarterly

$$\frac{SHLN}{S_t} = a \cdot \frac{H_t}{S_t} + b \cdot \frac{Prof}{S_t} + c \cdot i + e_t$$

No. of Observations	Period	Coefficients of			$\overline{R}^2$	Durbin-Watson Statistic	Mean of Depen. Variable	Std. Error of Regression
		a	b	c				
75	1958-1 1976-4	.3504** (.0569)	-.6373** (.0951)	1.160** (.1032)	.6898	.9555	.0770	.0189
44	1958-1 1968-4	-.0158 (.0708)	-.5240** (.1020)	2.414** (.2360)	.7389	1.2221	.0535	.0113
7	1969-1 1970-3	.4350 (.1576)	-.2701 (.1780)	.3504 (.4357)	.7730	2.2459	.1090	.0061
16	1970-4 1974-3	.3207** (.0402)	.3156* (.1423)	.0033 (.1320)	.6056	1.4496	.1110	.0085

(continued)

TABLE 23 (continued)

No. of Objects	Period	Coefficients of			$\overline{R^2}$	Durbin-Watson Statistic	Mean of Depen. Variable	Std. Error of Regression
		a	b	c				
9	1974-4 1976-4	-.1854 (.3273)	.3740 (.4028)	1.227 (.5387)	.4756	1.9051	.1039	.0189

[a] Standard errors (in parentheses).

[b] * and ** mark coefficients significant at the 5 percent and 1 percent levels of significance.

[c] $\dfrac{SHLN}{S_t} = \dfrac{\text{Short-Term Debt}}{\text{Sales}}$.

[d] $\dfrac{H_t}{S_t} = \dfrac{\text{Finished Goods Inventory}}{\text{Sales}}$.

[e] $\dfrac{Prof}{S_t} = \dfrac{\text{\$ Earnings Before Tax}}{\text{Sales}} = \text{Profit Margin}$.

[f] i = Interest rates on short-term business loans, annual rate (expressed in hundreths).

SOURCE: Bureau of the Census, H_t, S_t, for Industry 28; FTC Quarterly Report, SHLN and Prof for Industry 28; NBER FY35R Series, interest rates on short-term business loans.

sign for "c" would have been indicative that firms tend to borrow more when interest rates are (attractively) low, and less borrowing as they are higher. Actually, as a glance at table 22 shows, the reverse is more nearly the case with higher interest rates accompanying more borrowing—i.e., interest rates reflect, in good part, demand for credit.

The significant "b" and "c" coefficients for period I (1958-1–1968-4) lend further support to this interpretation. The negative sign for "a" is not important in view of the small size of the coefficient and its appreciably larger standard error—in fact, for practical purposes, a $\sim$ 0, and the more important point is that up until 1969 H_t/S_t was not an important determinant of the chemical industry's needs for short-term credit.

Period II (1969-1–1970-3) was characterized by growth of H_t/S_t, and (as table 22 shows), declining profit margin, and an increase in short-term debt. Coefficient "a," which narrowly misses being significant at the 5 percent level, and "b" are consistent with these observations; "c" is nonsignificant.

During period III (1970-4–1974-3), chemical firms pursued inventory reductions. The period showed some improvements in profit margins, but ended on another downbeat. Short-term debt levels declined slightly, but showed more variability than in the period preceding. The significant (at 1 percent) "a" coefficient is consistent, but very interestingly, the sign of the significant "b" coefficient has been reversed. One might reasonably suspect that, during a period of credit tightness, borrowing reflected "credit-worthiness" to a greater extent than need for short-term credit. That "c" is essentially zero is consistent with the latter point.

For the final period, inventory ratios were held at lower level; and, according to table 22, the short-term debt ratio averaged lower than during the preceding two periods, but it was substantially more variable. Consistent with this, "c" again tends to demonstrate interest rates tending to accompany loan volume. However, as the lower $\bar{R}^2$ and higher standard error of the regression demonstrate, loan volume was variable—nevertheless, while chemical firms may have continued to need short-term credit, it appears from the low H_t/S_t ratio maintained during period IV, that efforts were made to reduce the need.

We can conclude a number of useful points from this analysis of the chemical industry. While the finished goods/sales ratio, H_t/S_t did remain *more or less* constant over the 1958–1976 period, both seasonal and secular variations were noted. With respect to the latter, the overall test period was separated into four individual sub-periods during which treatment of H_t/S_t by chemical firms showed significant differences. Further, the changes were shown to be consistent with financial factors, using a simple model.

What has not been demonstrated so far is that such changes necessarily represent profit-maximizing behavior. The task addressed in the next several chapters of this study will be to extend the analysis in this direction.

7

Timing and Seasonal Behavior

The basic question addressed in this chapter is "how quick and accurate are manufacturers' adjustments of production levels when demand changes?" A corollary question relates to the extent that finished goods inventories serve as *buffers* for short-term changes in demand.

One of the strategic assumptions made earlier (see chapter 5, note 9), in development of the Belsley model for a profit-maximizing level of production, was that there was a natural time period over which manufacturers reacted to changes in new order levels. It is our present objective to see if this can be determined for the industries studied. Could reaction be quick (and accurate) enough that essentially no lag in response existed (almost as if manufacturers had foreknowledge of orders to be received)? Or, are two quarter lags in response typical, as has been concluded from various empirical studies?[1]

To some extent, the answers will tell us something of *how* decisions are made, as well as *how quickly*. For example, if we were to find that the manufacturers in a given industry had already set P_t (and we note that P_t, in general, needs to be planned in advance) at a level which closely coincided with N_t, new orders received during the period; then, if the period were as short as a month, we could infer that production plans were set *in advance* of receipt of orders for the month. In turn, this would suggest a picture along the following lines: (1) customers are continuing (not sporadic) users of the product(s), though their level of usage may vary;[2] (2) close and continuing liaison exists between the purchasing function of users and the marketing function of producers, on the formers' anticipated needs during the forthcoming period.

On the other hand, the longer the reaction time, the more likely it would seem either that the production process itself was a lengthy one (as was indicated in chapter 6 for the durable goods industries studied); or, that manufacturers' expectations were based largely (or solely) on previously realized sales of goods—in other words, a lagged production response.

Production to Stock: Timing of Response to New Orders

The latter of the two possibilities mentioned above could possibly apply to production to stock, which we will examine first. For this method of manufacture, we have the relation (from 4.1) repeated here:

$$P_t = S_t + DH_t \qquad (\text{with } S_t = N_t) \tag{7.1}$$

The most direct test of performance is suggested by the fact that if DH were to equal zero, (7.1) would simply reduce to:

$$P_t = S_t = N_t \tag{7.2}$$

On the other hand, if manufacturers were to respond in lagged fashion, we should find that P_t would fit better with order levels of one, or more, periods previous. For the sake of being complete, there is also the scenario (if Say's Law were to hold) that current sales depended on the production level of a previous period—i.e., equivalent to P_t correlating best with order levels of some period ahead.

Therefore a regression test is indicated of the form:

$$P_t = a \cdot N_i + e_i \tag{7.3}$$

where the subscript (i) indicates testing of new orders, both current, and for periods ahead or behind (i.e., leads or lags). For example, testing for two periods' lagged dependence on new orders would be written:

$$P_t = a \cdot N_{t-2} + e'_t \tag{7.4}$$

And, if the test were for a current relationship (with no lead or lag), it would be:

$$P_t = a \cdot N_t + e_t \tag{7.5}$$

We can assist the interpretation of the test results to be obtained by (briefly) comparing the structure of (7.5) with (7.1). Actually, this is slightly easier to do if we first rewrite (7.5) as:

$$P_t = (1)N_t + (a - 1)N_t + e_t \tag{7.5a}$$

And, it is clear that $(a - 1)N_t$ is, in fact, the counterpart of the DH term in (7.1). More precisely, by subtracting N_t from both sides of the equation (7.5a), we have:

$$DH_t = (a - 1)N_t + e_t \tag{7.6}$$

Therefore, we would expect that:

1. The mean value of $(a - 1)N_t$ should closely approximate DH_t; i.e., $(a - 1)\bar{N}_t = \overline{DH_t}$.

2. The standard error of the test regression,[3]

$$\frac{\sum\limits_{T-1}^{t} e_t^2}{}$$

should approximately equal the standard deviation of DH_t; i.e.,

$$\frac{\sum(DH - DH_t)^2}{T - 1} = \frac{\sum\limits^{t} e_t^2}{T - 1}$$

where $T =$ the number of monthly observations.

3. Of course, a would be expected to approximate unity.

Table 24 shows the mean values, standard deviations, and correlation of month-to-month changes in P_t, S_t, and H_t, or, DP, DS, and DH, for the four industries producing only to stock.

It is worth noting (on table 24) that the mean values of DP and DS are approximately equal in each of the four cases, and that DH is smaller—perhaps 20–60 percent of the size of the first two. In three of the four cases, the correlation between DP and DS is good, but these variables are only very little related to DH. Industry 21 comes to the rescue, however, by demonstrating that this observation is only "generally true," and is not a generalization.

The other question of importance is "what will be the best data base to use in testing?" Monthly (unadjusted) data would seem the choice on two counts:

1. Monthly data is the shortest period for which data are available. Since we are addressing the question of "how quickly ...?" the shorter the test period, the better.

2. Seasonally adjusted data would offer the apparent advantage that seasonal perturbations have been removed from consideration. Unfortunately, manufacturers' adjustments to seasonal changes in demand are part and package of the overall decision process, and eliminating them may not be the sort of help we need.

There is also the consideration that the moving average seasonal smoothing process (BuCensus uses m-9 and m-10) builds in precisely what our

Table 24.   Month-to-Month Changes in Production, Sales, and Finished Goods, and their Correlation Matrices for Production to Stock Industries: 1958-1976

	Means ($\bar{M}$)	SD		Correlation Matrix		
				DP	DH	DS
Ind. 20	46.1	366.7	DP	1.000	.3445	.9270
	23.4	142.2	DH		1.000	.1758
	46.9	332.3	DS			1.000
Ind. 21	1.94	47.6	DP	1.000	.6752	.4647
	1.17	29.9	DH		1.000	.0709
	1.93	27.6	DS			1.000
Ind. 28	34.8	240.0	DP	1.000	-.1115	.9721
	17.8	65.7	DH		1.000	-.2197
	34.8	263.8	DS			1.000
Ind. 29	30.0	110.3	DP	1.000	.3156	.9224
	6.1	38.5	DH		1.000	.1086
	29.3	103.7	DS			1.000

NOTE: DP $= P_t - P_{t-1} =$ change in production from previous month, $\$\bar{M}$; DH $= H_t - H_{t-1} =$ change in finished goods inventories, $\$\bar{M}$; DS $= S_t - S_{t-1} =$ change in sales from previous month, $\$\bar{M}$.

test is constructed to detect—i.e., a dependence of P_t on a lagging or leading relationship with sales.

And, with no further ado, we can turn to inspection of the results of OLSQ regression tests on equation (7.3). The results are shown in table 25, and we have a number of observations to make:

1. As expected, the coefficient (a) has a value slightly greater than unity when the current period P_t and N_t are the variables tested. And, because of the overall growth of each industry over the 1958–1976 period, the size of the coefficient is incrementally larger for each additional month new orders (sales) are lagged—this is equivalent to saying that somewhat smaller sales figures need to be multiplied by slightly larger coefficients to equate them

to *current* production. The reverse is true, naturally, for observations on leading months.

2. The relations between the standard error of the regression and the standard deviation of DH over the test period are close, as expected, for the regression results on the current period variables, for each of the industries. Similarly, the comparison of the mean value of DH to be inferred from $(a - 1)N_t$, and the computed values for $\overline{DH}$ is close.

	Industry 20	Industry 21	Industry 28	Industry 29
Standard error of the regression	141.5	29.9	65.2	38.2
SD of DH	142.2	29.9	65.7	38.5
$(a - 1) \cdot \overline{N}_t$	26.0	1.29	17.5	7.52
$\overline{DH}$	23.3	1.17	17.8	6.10

3. The remaining statistics shown on table 25 are: (a) the standard error of coefficient (a); (b) the *t* statistic for the coefficient—or more formally, the *t* statistic for rejection of the null hypothesis that a = 0; and (c) $\overline{R}^2$ for the regression.

    Looking first at the test results for the current period, we see that the indications show very good fit for three of the industries; the $\overline{R}^2$'s are excellent, and the standard errors for the coefficient are low and, hence, the *t* statistics are high, indicating a very high degree of confidence in rejection of the null hypothesis.

    Industry 21 saves us from too great an effort of self-congratulation, but even in this case, both the *t* statistic and the $\overline{R}^2$ value indicate a fairly good fit. However, the less strong relationship between P_t and N_t in this case was somewhat foreshadowed by the correlation results of table 24 for the tobacco industry.

4. However, by far the most provocative observation is the symmetrical pattern, for each industry (the case for Industry 21 being weaker), by which the statistics vary one, two, and three months away from the current period results. The standard errors increase in tandem (almost), as one moves a month further from the current (N_t) result column, and in exactly the same fashion, the $\overline{R}^2$ and *t* statistic results decrease in tandem.

    With these results, which it would not be unfair to call "bell-shaped," we are being told several things at once.

    (a) Not only do the results point strongly to the fit of P_t and N_t as being better than any lead/lag relation, but the symmetry of the pattern helps to estimate whether the current period is "right on" in timing, or offset in one direction or another. If the latter were the case, the

Table 25. A Regression Test of Dependence of Production on Timing of
New Orders, Production to Stock Industries (1958-1976), Monthly Data
(Unadjusted)

	N + 3	N + 2	N + 1	N_t	N − 1	N − 2	N − 3
Industry 20							
Coefficient	.9838	.9902	.9966	1.0031	1.0086	1.0137	1.0195
(Std. Error)	(.0040)	(.0036)	(.0025)	(.0010)	(.0028)	(.0037)	(.0041)
t Stat.	245.7	277.4	391.9	961.8	354.5	272.1	246.0
$\bar{R}^2$	.9720	.9781	.9891	.9982	.9867	.9775	.9725
Industry 21							
Coefficient	.9884	.9931	.9974	1.0029	1.0054	1.0102	1.0144
(Std. Error)	(.0061)	(.0054)	(.0050)	(.0042)	(.0060)	(.0058)	(.0058)
t Stat.	162.3	183.0	199.6	236.7	167.3	173.3	176.2
$\bar{R}^2$	.8499	.8825	.9016	.9308	.8617	.8710	.8752
Industry 28							
Coefficient	.9709	.9820	.9931	1.0042	1.0126	1.0206	1.0300
(Std. Error)	(.0061)	(.0053)	(.0036)	(.0009)	(.0037)	(.0055)	(.0066)

(continued)

TABLE 25 (continued)

	N + 3	N + 2	N + 1	N_t	N - 1	N - 2	N - 3
t Stat.	159.5	186.4	273.4	1080.5	273.9	185.0	157.1
$\overline{R}^2$	.9533	.9662	.9844	.9990	.9846	.9663	.9534
Industry 29							
Coefficient	.9585	.9730	.9879	1.0030	1.0170	1.0313	1.0454
(Std. Error)	(.0034)	(.0027)	(.0021)	(.0008)	(.0023)	(.0030)	(.0039)
t Stat.	280.6	364.1	469.6	1257.8	445.0	341.0	267.1
$\overline{R}^2$	.9907	.9945	.9967	.9996	.9964	.9939	.9901

NOTE: E.g., N_i becomes N - 2, when i = -2, and the relation being tested is dependence of current production level on two months' lagged new orders.

SOURCE: Bureau of the Census, Manufacturers' Shipments, Inventories and Orders (1958-1976), monthly, unadjusted.

pattern would have been skewed, implying that one might roughly estimate the timing offset thereby. For example, for results in the N_t and N_{-1} column essentially similar, one might judge the results to be in the order of one-half month lagged, in terms of dependence on sales. Or, if the peak was clearly one month lagged, the signal would be that P_t depended on last month's new order level. The results for Industry 21 suggest, perhaps, that production in the tobacco industry depends on current sales predominantly, but with a bias toward next month's which is less than one-half a month; in other words, one might tentatively conclude that production leads sales by $\sim$ 1 week in this particular industry.

(b)   There is a basic question involved here about the "bell shapes" of the results. Does this mean, in three and one-half of the cases, that manufacturers setting P_t "just happen to" plan their production, in large measure, to coincide with current new orders (in a statistical-averaging sense)? Or is it more reasonable to think that they exert their best efforts toward making it happen? The writer leans toward the latter conclusion.

(c)   The generally accepted hypothesis of (up to two quarters) lag in manufacturers' response to changes in orders is not borne out. For these industries, at least, the evidence of the results points to businesses run in a manner that enables close estimation of sales volume for the current period, and concomitantly, closely matching levels of production.

d.   The above rationale suggests that we must more closely examine two topics:

(i) seasonal patterns and behavior, and

(ii) the extent to which manufacturers actually use H_t as a buffer stock for "unexpected changes in orders."

These will be pursued later in this chapter.

Production to Both Stock and Order: Timing of Response

We have a problem in performing a similar analysis on industries producing to both stock and order. Once again the lack of separability of the "to stock" and "to order" data intrudes; however, let us try.

From Equation (4.2) for production to order we had:

$$P_t^o = N_t^o - DU_t \tag{7.7}$$

If we add (8.1), $P_t^s = S_t^s + DH_t = N_t^o + DH_t$, the result is:

$$P_t = S_t + DH_t = N_t - DU_t + DH_t. \tag{7.8}$$

It would be tempting, at this point, to remark that if we assumed both DU and DH to be zero (for testing purposes), that, as in the preceding analysis, we could test for lead/lag/current relationship between P_t and N_t. However, it would appear that we are asking twice as much to equate *two* variables with zero without better reason than simple enthusiasm.

However, if we rearrange (7.8) we would have:

$$N_t = P_t + DU_t - DH_t, \tag{7.9}$$

and similarly,

$$N_{t-1} = P_{t-1} + DU_{t-1} - DH_{t-1}. \tag{7.9a}$$

Noting that $DN_t = N_t - N_{t-1}$, if we add DN_t to both sides of (7.9a):

$$N_t = P_{t-1} + DN_t + DU_{t-1} - DH_{t-1}. \tag{7.10}$$

Substitution of the right hand side of (7.10) into equation (7.8) to replace N_t provides a somewhat more elaborate appearance:

$$P_t = P_{t-1} + DN_t + DU_{t-1} - DH_{t-1} - DU_t + DH_t. \tag{7.11}$$

Now, it would appear more reasonable to assume zero values for test purposes for the last two terms in view of the information already present in the relation on: previous production level, and previous levels of unfilled orders and finished goods inventories, *plus* the information on change in level of new orders. In other words, we propose to do precisely what was thought of before with (7.8); but now it looks more plausible, because of the bouquet of information contained in N_t per equation (7.10). So, our regression test relation would again be:

$$P_t = a \cdot N_i + \epsilon_t \tag{7.12}$$

Once again, we intend to test P_t data against leading, lagging, and current new orders. However, this time (remembering the likelihood of slower changes in production level of industries with sizeable stocks of work-in-process and of unfilled orders), we will provide up to *six* months' lag in the new orders tested. In fact, to make sure that sufficient time span has been provided, we intend to perform the same test with *quarterly* (unadjusted) data as well.

These test results are presented in tables 26 and 27 respectively. Not too surprisingly, the pattern presented has a somewhat different appearance.

One of the first differences to be noted in examination of the new set of test results, is that the current period ($P_t : N_t$) coefficients are somewhat smaller than those of Table 25. The difference is symptomatic of the disparate nature of the production to order function, and that of production to stock. From equation (7.8) we know the $P_t > N_t$, only if $DU_t < DH_t$. A list of the mean quarterly values of the latter two variables over the test period shows:

	DU ($,$\bar{M}$)	DH ($,$\bar{M}$)
Industry 26	21.7	21.8
Industry 27	7.4	14.2
Industry 34	247	45.6
Industry 35	512	78
Industry 36	224	42.2

Therefore, we can anticipate a current period coefficient for Industry 27 which, like those of table 25, is slightly greater than one. Industry 26 ought to have a coefficient very close to unity, and the rest somewhat less than one. This, of course, does not mean a lack of growth of the latter industries over the 1958–1976 period; rather, the simple fact (i.e., by definition) that these industries produce a substantial part of their output *after* receipt of orders. Logically, this means that the coefficient will not equal *one* until the period of (lagging) activity in which production catches up with unfilled orders.

In fact, as a qualitative difference between the "to order" and "to stock" production functions, the relative size of DU and DH, respectively, gives a useful signal. However, we have no quantitative basis, unfortunately, on which we can say "this is the relative proportion of each function," as a firm measure of the contribution of each type of activity to overall industry performance (though naturally, the higher the proportion of DU/DH, the more production we may expect to order).

The ($P_t : N_t$) coefficients for Industries 26 and 27 conform to expectations in having values close to unity. The others (Industries 34, 35, and 36) are less than one as expected. From a timing response standpoint, Industries 26 and 34 seem to show a slight lag (i.e., a small fraction of a month), and Industry 27 something approaching one-half a month. From table 27, Industry 36 may lag one-quarter in production response, and Industry 35 as much as three-four quarters.

However, just what do we mean by "adjustment of the production level to a change in new orders" where production to order is involved? Something different, certainly, from the average length of unfilled orders (i.e., as expressed in days), which shows how long the average customer must wait after placing an order for a product made to order. Nor is there any direct connection necessarily, with the number of months one must wait until the production level equals the volume of new orders received in some previous month (i.e., a coefficient of one on table 26).[4] We must picture instead the situation existing at some point in time, with orders coming in at some given rate, and production going on at a (probably different) rate. If there were *no changes at all* in forthcoming months in the volume of new orders coming in, adjustment would be occurring in the length of time it took for inventory and unfilled orders accumulation (decumulation) to subside to negligible levels (i.e., production to adjust to order level), and we would essentially have $P_t = N_t$.

But really, there is never a month in which new orders do not change, and our question relates *not* to how long it would take the industry (or firm) to asymptotically approach a steady state equilibrium; but rather, we are considering whatever adjustment (Y) will be made *because* of the next change, and how long (on average) must we wait for the adjustment? As the question is phrased, Y is a function of the change in new orders (DN), so:

$$Y = f(DN), \tag{7.13}$$

and we have asked, in effect, "how long it takes for Y to happen?" However, and more explicitly, we are dealing with a large number of y_i's, or:

$$Y = \epsilon \ y_i \tag{7.14}$$

and

$$y_i = f(dn_i) \tag{7.15}$$

where y_i represents the adjustment for one particular firm (or product line), and the values of the y_i's are probably time dependent as well.

All this sounds fearfully complicated, but clearly production schedules *are* adjusted, and there is *some length period* for which we find that new production levels best correlate with new orders. The fit is not as sharply marked for industries producing largely to order, i.e., those at the bottom of tables 26 and 27, Industries 34, 35, and 36, as for those producing more, or altogether, to stock.

Industry 35, on table 27, best demonstrates the characteristics sketched out above of a collection of lagged adjustments, by the broad plateau which stretches over lagged values of new orders for two, three, and four quarters. Industry 36 has a similar plateau centering on a one-quarter lagged relation with new orders. On the other hand, Industry 34 shows relatively prompt response of adjustment of the production level to new orders. This difference in responses between industries is particularly interesting if one remembers

Table 26. A Regression Test of Dependence of Production on Timing of New Orders, for Industries Producing to both Stock and Order, 1958-1976, Monthly Data (Unadjusted)

	N_{+3}	N_{+2}	N_{+1}	N_t	N_{-1}	N_{-2}	N_{-3}	N_{-4}	N_{-5}	N_{-6}
				Industry 26						
Coef.	.9750	.9834	.9916	.9997	1.0055	1.0124	1.0120			
S. Er.	.0047	.0047	.0041	.0014	.0036	.0042	.0046			
t Stat.	206	210	244	717	281	242	221			
R^2	.9666	.9680	.9764	.9973	.9823	.9762	.9714			
				Industry 27						
Coef.	.978	.985	.993	1.001	1.006	1.011	1.018			
S. Er.	.0056	.0050	.0037	.0011	.0036	.0050	.0057			
t Stat.	175.6	197.9	269.4	923.0	281.8	201.3	178.3			
R^2	.9406	.9535	.9751	.9979	.9774	.9558	.9436			

(continued)

TABLE 26 (continued)

	N+3	N+2	N+1	N_t	N_{-1}	N_{-2}	N_{-3}	N_{-4}	N_{-5}	N_{-6}
Industry 34
Coef.	.954	.961	.970	.980	.987	.993	1.000	1.007		
S. Er.	.0067	.0068	.0059	.0039	.0057	.0063	.0069	.0073		
t Stat.	142.5	140.7	164.6	248.3	174.5	158.1	145.6	137.1		
R^2	.9256	.9244	.9450	.9760	.9515	.9411	.9305	.9215		
Industry 35
Coef.	.941	.951	.959	.969	.977	.985	.993	.999	1.007	1.015
S. Er.	.0105	.0100	.0101	.0095	.0102	.0105	.0108	.0078	.0080	.0072
t Stat.	89.9	94.6	94.6	102.1	95.5	94.2	92.1	127.4	125.2	141.5
R^2	.8610	.8749	.8756	.8936	.8789	.8755	.8698	.9311	.9286	.9439
Industry 36
Coef.	.959	.964	.971	.981	.985	.993	.999	1.004	1.011	1.018
S. Er.	.0064	.0074	.0063	.0044	.0063	.0059	.0058	.0067	.0067	.0057
t Stat.	151.0	131.0	154.8	223.0	155.3	168.1	172.9	150.1	151.4	178.8
R^2	.9226	.8983	.9272	.9651	.9282	.9383	.9413	.9219	.9229	.9441

Table 27. A Regression Test of Dependence of Production on Timing of New Orders, for Industries Producing to both Stock and Order, 1958-1976, Quarterly Data (Unadjusted)

Industry 26

	N_{+3}	N_{+2}	N_{+1}	N_t	N_{-1}	N_{-2}	N_{-3}	N_{-4}	N_{-5}	N_{-6}
Coef.	.926	.951	.997	.99945	1.024	1.050	1.078			
S. Er.	.0080	.0074	.0051	.0017	.0039	.0070	.0083			
t Stat.	115.9	128.6	191.2	600.6	259.7	150.6	122.6			
R^2	.9650	.9715	.9871	.9987	.9930	.9793	.9687			

Industry 27

	N_{+3}	N_{+2}	N_{+1}	N_t	N_{-1}	N_{-2}	N_{-3}	N_{-4}	N_{-5}	N_{-6}
Coef.	.943	.963	.980	1.001	1.019	1.038	1.059	1.080	1.097	1.115
S. Er.	.0063	.0055	.0061	.0012	.0061	.0058	.0072	.0047	.0081	.0072
t Stat.	148.8	175.8	159.7	828.7	167.8	179.1	146.3	229.1	135.1	153.8
R^2	.9710	.9797	.9759	.9991	.9786	.9810	.9715	.9883	.9663	.9739

(continued)

TABLE 27 (continued)

	N_{+3}	N_{+2}	N_{+1}	N_t	N_{-1}	N_{-2}	N_{-3}	N_{-4}	N_{-5}	N_{-6}
					Industry 34					
Coef.	.916	.935	.957	.981	1.003	1.022	1.040	1.060		
S. Er.	.0111	.0105	.0082	.0059	.0081	.0103	.0110	.0121		
$\underline{t}$ Stat.	82.4	88.9	117.0	166.0	123.4	99.2	94.9	87.7		
R^2	.9230	.9345	.9627	.9820	.9674	.9495	.9447	.9350		
					Industry 35					
Coef.	.901	.924	.951	.978	1.003	1.016	1.038	1.060	1.083	1.105
S. Er.	.0163	.0151	.0133	.0116	.0135	.0114	.0114	.0113	.0149	.0167
$\underline{t}$ Stat.	55.2	61.4	71.6	84.7	74.0	69.2	91.4	93.4	72.7	66.3
R^2	.8726	.8976	.9257	.9477	.9317	.9525	.9545	.9565	.9286	.9142
					Industry 36					
Coef.	.924	.943	.962	.982	1.002	1.020	1.038	1.054	1.073	1.089
S. Er.	.0101	.0086	.0072	.0061	.0058	.0069	.0091	.0114	.0127	.0139
$\underline{t}$ Stat.	91.8	109.7	132.9	161.5	171.7	148.5	114.4	92.9	84.5	78.1
R^2	.9266	.9493	.9660	.9774	.9796	.9723	.9529	.9278	.9120	.8959

(from table 18) that the latter three industries showed *relatively similar holdings of unfilled orders*—in other words, we are differentiating between the length of time required *to fill orders* and the apparent quickness (or slowness) toward changing rate of production in response to changes in the rate at which new orders are received.

We can add a small amount of additional perspective to this story by differentiating between the elements which make up N_t (per equation 7.10). In other words, instead of a regression test of the type $P_t = a \cdot N_t + e_t$, we would have, instead,

$$P_t = a_1 \cdot P_{t-1} + a_2 \cdot DN_t + a_3 \cdot DU_{t-1} + a_4 \cdot DH_{t-1} + e'_t \tag{7.16}$$

All coefficients have the sign which would be expected from (7.10), and in all but one case, the coefficients are significant at the 1 percent level or better.

In each case, in table 28, the dominant characteristic "determining" the current level of production is the level of production in the period just past—and interestingly, with approximately the same coefficient in each case. One would infer significant costs, in each case, to changes in the rate of production. In order, production of the three industries shows decreasing responsiveness to increases in new orders, but increasing response to any increase over the past period in unfilled orders.

We could rephrase this to say that there is a greater response at the top of the table to new (i.e., additional) business, and toward the bottom of the table, more concern about "getting behind" on unfilled orders. It would be interesting to see, if these industries were being further investigated (e.g., on the pattern of, and tactics used in, competitive behavior utilized by firms in these industries), how well these inferences would serve as a frame of reference, i.e., competition on delivery times, etc. We wish the tests used could be stronger in terms of quantitative characterization, but separability of the "to stock" and "to order" functions would seem to be required for further progress in this direction.

Seasonal Behavior of Industries Producing to Stock

Frequently in economic analyses, use is made of seasonally adjusted data—usually with the expressed wish that "seasonal effects not interfere with the analysis." Manufacturers, of course, do not have this luxury. One of the variables with which they must cope are seasonal variations. On occasion, people who do not have to deal with seasonal variation may well think that the phrase deals with a procession of events as predictable as the orbits of planets. However, those engaged in the seasonal adjustment of data (and, of course, businessmen who must cope with it) realize that everything is not necessarily cut and dried.

Table 28. A Regression Test of Equation (7.16): Dependence of Production on Lagged Production, and Changes in New Orders, Unfilled Orders (Lagged) and Inventory (Lagged), for Industries 26, 34, and 36, 1958-1976, Quarterly Data

| | Coefficient | | | |
	a_1	a_2	a_3	a_4
		Variable		
	P_{t-1}	DN_t	DU_{t-1}	DH_{t-1}
Ind. 26	1.004	.7214	.2330	-1.476
t Stat.	(188)	(7.1)	(.661)	(-2.7)
$\bar{R}^2 = .9930$				
Ind. 34	1.007	.5518	.3487	-.8262
t Stat.	(197)	(8.9)	(4.2)	(-2.3)
$\bar{R}^2 = .9916$				
Ind. 36	1.012	.4140	.4484	-2.409
t Stat.	(212)	(5.8)	(5.5)	(-6.6)

In this section we intend to investigate the seasonal behavior of the four industries in the study which produce to stock. The aim will be to see what patterns can be perceived, and, in particular, to address the question of the extent to which finished goods inventories are used as buffers for seasonal variations in demand.

The principal technique in seasonal adjustment of data is the use of moving-averaged data to replace the observations of individual periods. One could, of course, reverse the procedure, and study the departure of the data for each period from the "trend line." This approach, in other words, would focus on these first differences. An alternate approach has been used here, in which the data from monthly statistics have been segregated into a dozen sets (one for each month) for each industry, for the 1959–1976 period. The eighteen years' values for each of the variables (P_t, S_t, H_t, DP, DS, DH) were then averaged to obtain arithmetical means for each of the twelve calendar months.

To make sure there is no ambiguity, DP_7 (the change in July production) would show the increase (decrease) from June (i.e., $P_7 - P_6$) *and not* the change from the preceding July.

These results are presented in table 29, and figures 5 and 6 show the corresponding graphs for each industry of $\bar{P}_t$, $\bar{S}_t$, and $\bar{H}_t$. The useful attribute of

Table 29.   Seasonal Pattern of Four Industries Producing to Stock as Shown by Inter-Month Comparison of Mean Monthly Levels of Production, Sales, and Finished Goods, 1959-1976, Monthly Data (Unadjusted)

Month	Ind. 20			Ind. 21			Ind. 28			Ind. 29		
	$\overline{P}_t$	$\overline{S}_t$	$\overline{H}_t$	$\overline{P}_t$	$\overline{S}_t$	$\overline{H}_t$	$\overline{P}_t$	$\overline{S}_t$	$\overline{H}_t$	$\overline{P}_t$	$\overline{S}_t$	$\overline{H}_t$
January	7630	7647	4799	418	410	149	3781	3723	2736	2294	2318	1220
February	7930	8027	4702	431	420	159	4062	4011	2788	2378	2398	1200
March	7958	8047	4613	440	434	166	4190	4184	2794	2348	2349	1199
April	7987	7980	4620	441	431	175	4266	4292	2768	2394	2401	1192
May	8011	8025	4606	456	450	182	4203	4221	2750	2413	2405	1200
June	8312	8339	4579	469	477	174	4165	4164	2751	2542	2534	1208
July	7976	7972	4583	435	458	151	3834	3826	2759	2547	2513	1242
August	8534	8305	4812	472	469	155	4119	4112	2766	2615	2575	1282
September	8924	8742	4994	467	458	164	4287	4318	2735	2609	2586	1305
October	8942	8771	5165	489	459	194	4215	4194	2756	2607	2583	1329
November	8556	8533	5188	475	465	204	4054	3989	2821	2626	2622	1334
December	8229	8291	5126	418	460	162	3950	3851	2920	2654	2673	1315

NOTE: $\overline{P}_t$, $\overline{S}_t$ and $\overline{H}_t$ values in $, $\overline{M}$.

this approach is that it gives the average relation of each of the variables, for each of the calendar months, with each month's characteristics separately examinable. This begs the question, of course "is there actually a seasonal pattern to be observed"? That there at least *seems to be* strikes one when looking at graphs of the data which show repetitive sales peaks and valleys over a period of years (e.g., figure 4). The next obvious question would be on the consistency of seasonal patterns, which will be further examined below.

While this approach is useful, it has built-in characteristics for which some caveats are appropriate:

1. There is a tilt problem which stems from temporal growth of the industries. The chemical industry, for example has grown at an average rate of 9% over the period.[5] Hence the December figures show (almost) a nine percent higher level of activity than January's. Or, to rephrase this, to see how things would change from December to the following month would require a second set of January data to have been established with a "year later"

Figure 5.   Mean Monthly Values of Production, Sales, and Finished Goods Inventories ($, M̄) (1959-1976)

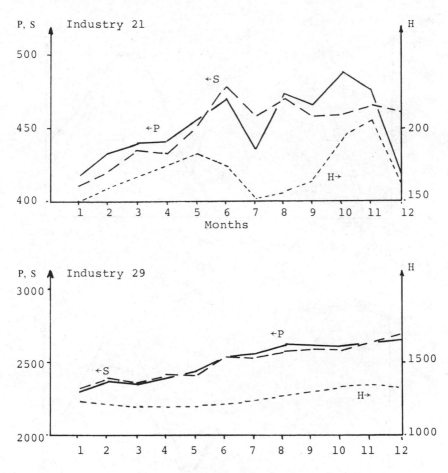

relation to the first January set. For the present study, this step has not been deemed necessary, but recognizing that there is a tilt is prudent.

2. If an industry were to have shown zero growth over the test period, the standard deviations of the variables would be very useful in characterizing how closely followed was the seasonal pattern in any given month. Small deviations would clearly indicate a closely followed repetitive pattern— and, au revers. However, given industry growth, the standard deviations largely reflect simple changes in size, and have relatively, little utility for analysis.[6]

Figure 6. Mean Monthly Values of Production, Sales, and Finished Goods Inventories ($, M̄) (1959-1976)

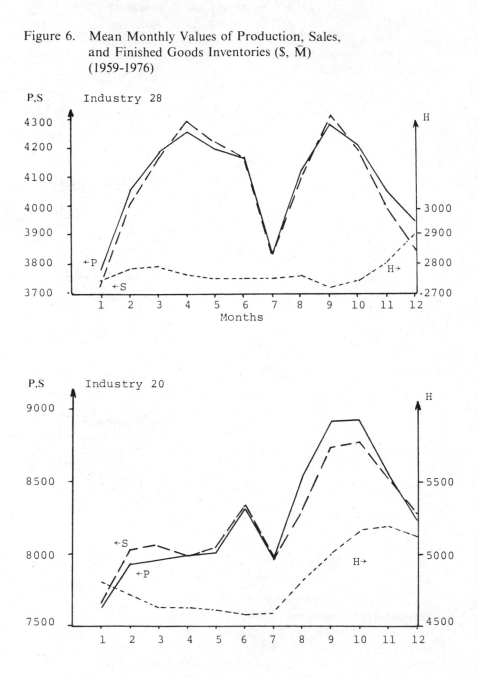

3. Lastly, DH has a dual identity. It is, at the same time, the change from the level of finished goods inventory at the end of last month to the level at the end of this month, *and* the difference this month between levels of P_t and S_t.

Other things being equal (e.g., if S_t were considered for the moment to be fixed), the more P_t were to increase, the larger DH would be. Hence a built in tendency for DH to correlate positively with DP. Alternatively, with P_t for the moment fixed, a positive DS would mean a negative DH, or a built in tendency for a negative DS:DH correlation.

From an overall standpoint, each of the four industries shows seasonal patterns which are more or less strongly marked, though differing individually. Figures 5 and 6 show the seasonal peaks and valleys (or lack of them) better than the written word, but for the moment we will defer description of the characteristics of the individual industries.

The most immediate observation, from both the graphs and the numerical data of table 29, is that sales and production levels are very closely related, and, not too surprisingly, are of very similar magnitude. It would also seem that some sort of relation exists between sales (or production, for that matter) and finished goods inventories, but just what is not immediately evident.

To help unravel this, an additional tool is useful. Correlation coefficients have been calculated for P_t, S_t, and H_t, and also for their monthly changes (DP, DS, DH) for each calendar month over the 1959–1976 period, for the four industries under examination. To reduce the bulk of the resulting tabulation as an aid to comparison, these results have been summarized in table 30 by showing simply the range (i.e., the single highest and lowest monthly values) and the mean correlation coefficients, for each of the twelve months, for $P_t:S_t$, $S_t:H_t$, DP:DS, and DS:DH. For the latter two pairings, some though not all of the correlation coefficients are negative, and the means of positive and negative coefficients are separately reported.

It turns out that the correlation of mean monthly rates of production and sales ($P_t:S_t$) is extremely close indeed, with coefficients just barely under unity for Industries 20, 28, and 29, and only slightly lower for Industry 21. The correlation between sales and finished goods inventories ($S_t:H_t$) is generally good, though pale in comparison with the $P_t:S_t$ results.

Monthly changes in production and sales (DP:DS) have a fair to good positive correlation. However, the correlation of month to month changes in finished goods inventories with sales changes (DS:DH) is erratic. The single best correlation is represented by a negative coefficient of .9274 (Industry 28, November), while for other months for the same industry, the range of coefficients extends as far as a positive .2498 (for January).

That some of the DS:DH coefficients are negative is not unexpected because, as mentioned earlier, there is this built-in tendency. However, the

Table 30. Correlation Coefficients for Monthly Production and Sales,
for Sales and Finished Goods Inventories, and for their Month to Month
Changes, of Industries Producing to Stock, 1959-1976, Monthly Data
(Unadjusted)

	Ind. 20		Ind. 21		Ind. 28		Ind. 29	
	P:S	S:H	P:S	S:H	P:S	S:H	P:S	S:H
Highest	+.9998	+.9866	+.9954	+.9368	+.9999	+.9791	+.9999	+.9907
Lowest	+.9994	+.9703	+.9513	+.8121	+.9994	+.9475	+.9996	+.9523
Mean	+.9996	+.9805	+.9802	+.8686	+.9997	+.9637	+.9998	+.9742
Number of (+) Coefficients	12	12	12	12	12	12	12	12

	DP:DS	DS:DH	DP:DS	DS:DH	DP:DS	DS:DH	DP:DS	DP:DH
Highest	+.9629	+.4939	+.8737	+.5524	+.9873	+.2498	+.9847	+.5681
Lowest	+.6703	-.5102	-.0239	-.3746	+.8317	-.9274	+.6913	-.4662
Mean of (+) Coefficients	+.8765	+.3415	+.5826	+.3184	+.9158	+.1890	+.8810	+.3108
Number of (+) Coefficients	12	7	11	5	12	3	12	7
Mean of (−) Coefficients	----	-.2243	-.0239	-.1644	----	-.4343	----	-.2308
Number of (−) Coefficients	0	5	1	7	0	9	0	5

coefficients are decidedly not uniformly negative, probably because (as can be calculated from table 29) there are appreciable changes over the calendar year in the ratio of finished goods to sales (i.e., H_t/S_t). The tobacco industry, for example, shows a change in the H_t/S_t ratio of 29 percent over an average year, while the petroleum industry's ratio varies but a third as much. The food and chemical industries are in between with 14 percent and 18 percent respectively. The significance of the observation for our present purposes lies not in inter-industry comparison, but rather in helping examine the manner in which finished goods inventories are used over a period of seasonally changing demand. (At the latter part of chapter 6, three examples were given of how and why changes of inventory pattern occur over a period of years, so we already know that changes/variation do not stem only from seasonal behaviour characteristics.)

The most common explanations for the holding of finished goods inventories are the familiar "buffer" motive, and that of production-smoothing. Our immediate task is to determine if either premise is supported by the data.

While the two explanations sound different, they turn out to be opposite sides of a coin. For the former, additional (fewer) goods required by an unexpected increase (decrease) in sales are provided by inventory decumulation (accumulation), rather than a change in rate of production. In the latter case, rather than change the rate of production (and incur the costs of doing so) the additional (fewer) goods required by anticipated changes in sales are provided by inventory decumulation (accumulation). Save for "unexpected" vs. "anticipated," the two statements say much the same thing, albeit with slightly different emphasis. For either, confirmation that one (or both) of these motives were providing the primary impetus for changes in the level of finished goods inventories would be signalled by two observations. First, month to month changes for S_t and H_t should be of comparable size and opposite sign (i.e., we would expect a good negative correlation of DH and DS); secondly, the month to month changes of P_t should be relatively smaller than, and have no particular relation to, changes in S_t (i.e., very little correlation between DP and DS).

However, something quite different is shown by table 30. There is decidedly not a good negative correlation between DH and DS, unless one could base the entire case on the isolated result for Industry 28's November coefficient of $-.9274$ (with next best support offered by the same industry's October coefficient of $-.6633$). Besides that, the correlation between month to month changes in sales and production is positive, and sufficiently strong for Industries 20, 28, and 29, *not only to negate the buffer/production smoothing explanation, but to reasonably support the alternative premise* that for these industries the primary means of adjustment to change in sales is a corresponding change in rate of production.

Additional substantiation of this conclusion is provided by relative sizes of the mean month to month changes of P_t, S_t, and H_t. Listed below are the means of DP, DS, and DH, calculated on an absolute basis (i.e., irrespective of whether the change is positive or negative), to avoid misinterpretation of an average of large plus and minus changes as a small number. For the four industries over the 1959–1976 period, the means of each, in millions of dollars, are:

	$\overline{DP}$	$\overline{DS}$	$\overline{DH}$
Industry 20	230	214	77
Industry 21	20.8	12.9	12.9
Industry 28	158	185	25
Industry 29	36.3	43.2	15.5

With the tobacco industry once more providing an exception, mean month to month inventory changes are appreciably smaller than the corresponding changes in sales, while the mean production changes approximately correspond in magnitude to sales changes. This is additional evidence against either the buffer or production-smoothing hypotheses, and supports the premise that changes in production rate are the primary means of adjustment to seasonal changes in sales for industries producing to stock.

Nor do the Industry 21 results help the buffer/production-smoothing argument; for, while $\overline{DS}$ and $\overline{DH}$ are equivalent in size, $\overline{DP}$ instead of being obligingly smaller is actually 60 percent larger. We would need to see larger changes in $\overline{DH}$ than $\overline{DP}$ to be able to identify the results as production-smoothing (or buffering).

To regroup for a moment, it *is* clear, from inspection of the graphs of figures 5 and 6 and the data of table 29, that there is a tendency for finished goods inventories to be built up in advance of periods of stronger sales, and to be run down during them. However, neither buffering nor production-smoothing can be concluded to be the major mechanism at work. An alternative thesis is needed to explain how inventories are used by industries producing to stock. This topic will be pursued at the end of the chapter.

Turning next to inspection of the seasonal characteristics of the individual industries, Industry 29 shows the least variability between "most active" and "least active" months. The very largest changes in month-to-month sales are only three to five percent of sales levels during January/February (heating oil season) and May/June, respectively. One tends normally to think of seasonal characteristics as something synonomous with the profile of a mountain range, but in this case there are no real "peaks." Instead, there is a pattern of steady inventory accumulation which goes on from May through November (with an August maximum in rate of accumulation), and a drawing down of inventories during the winter months.

This brings us back to a question earlier raised. We might very well wonder at this point whether the absence of seasonal sales (and production) peaks in the petroleum industry's graph is a signal that there is not a distinctive seasonal pattern at all. Perhaps, instead of a repetitive pattern, we are simply looking at the relatively flat profile resulting from averaging eighteen years of annually variable behavior.

To test this possibility, an OLSQ regression was examined for each industry, and for each calendar month over the 1959–1976 period, of the relation:

$$H_t = a + b \cdot S_t + \epsilon_t \tag{7.17}$$

The coefficient "b" has a family resemblance to the H_t/S_t ratio, although the presence of "a" complicates its interpretation in this manner. However, the real merit of this approach is that differences between the coefficients of the various months would be indicative of seasonal differences. Further, the coefficients and differences between them can be tested for significance by using their standard errors (or, the "t" statistics derived from the standard errors). Complete tabulation of these regression results would be bulky, and to facilitate comparison again, a summary is given. Table 31 shows only the values of the coefficient "b" and its accompanying "t" statistic for each of the calendar months.[7]

In spite of the somewhat featureless annual pattern of the petroleum industry (figure 5), the relatively high "t" statistics for the coefficients of the regression test results of table 31 for Industry 29 testify to a definite seasonality. For instance, we can test to see if the null hypothesis can be rejected that the population mean for the "b" coefficients of two different months is the same. Such a test for January and August yields a test statistic, $t = 4.47$—appreciably better than required to reject the null hypothesis at the 1 percent level on a two-tailed test. Nor is the significance of the result restricted to a test involving January (which has the highest average H_t/S_t ratio). An August/October comparison produces a test statistic, $t = 4.86$, with similar result.

Turning to Industry 20, its most intriguing characteristic (as shown on figure 6) is the pattern of P_t exceeding S_t by about 7 percent during August–October, during which 95 percent of all finished goods inventories buildup takes place. The pattern is reversed from December through March when inventory depletion takes place. One might infer that this sort of a pattern has something to do, for the food industry, with the timing and availability of crops which provide the industry's raw materials. A test of the regression results for the "b" coefficients of August (at the beginning of inventory buildup) and November (at its end), along the same lines as above, yields a test

Table 31.   Summary of Regression Test Results of: $H_t = a + b \cdot S_t + \epsilon_t$ for Industries Producing to Stock, 1959-1976, Monthly Data (Unadjusted)

Month	Ind. 20	Ind. 21	Ind. 28	Ind. 29
January	.535 (.0298) 18.0	.806 (.1061) 7.6	.679 (.0375) 18.1	.226 (.0159) 14.2
February	.510 (.0268) 19.0	1.083 (.1350) 8.0	.593 (.0373) 15.9	.199 (.0146) 13.6
March	.508 (.0240) 21.2	.939 (.1345) 7.0	.558 (.0391) 14.3	.203 (.0152) 12.5
April	.502 (.0228) 22.1	.939 (.1534) 6.1	.533 (.0414) 12.9	.184 (.0133) 13.8
May	.495 (.0221) 22.4	.886 (.1577) 5.6	.560 (.0439) 12.8	.189 (.0118) 16.1
June	.466 (.0232) 20.1	.946 (.1292) 7.3	.539 (.0401) 13.4	.186 (.0094) 19.9
July	.478 (.0271) 17.6	.932 (.1272) 7.3	.609 (.0514) 11.9	.196 (.0100) 19.6
August	.475 (.0296) 16.0	.914 (.1210) 7.6	.567 (.0430) 13.2	.207 (.0085) 24.5
September	.481 (.0225) 21.4	1.011 (.1514) 6.7	.533 (.0383) 13.9	.215 (.0095) 22.6
October	.492 (.0239) 20.6	.856 (.1164) 7.4	.577 (.0401) 14.4	.220 (.0075) 29.1
November	.513 (.0213) 24.2	.929 (.1668) 5.6	.624 (.0326) 19.1	.213 (.0095) 22.3
December	.536 (.0252) 21.3	.927 (.0865) 10.7	.662 (.0344) 19.3	.207 (.0111) 18.7

NOTE: Each box shows the numerical results for:

Coefficient b   .535
(Standard Error)   (.0298)
t Statistic of Coeff. b   18.0

statistic, $t = 4.42$, and once more the hypothesis, that the samples were drawn from a common population, can be rejected.

Industry 21, of course, is a little different once again. From figure 5 it appears that there is significant inventory depletion in (only) two months, July and December—and the reason is markedly lower production in these months. Whether this is based on vacation practices of the industry, or reflects some other cause, is not our immediate concern. However, we would like to address the question of the confidence to be attached to these observations. Using, once more, the test of "b" coefficients for one of these months, July, and an "inventory building" month, October, we have a test statistic, $t = 1.872$. The results is similar to those above, but the rejection of the null hypothesis can now be made only with 90 percent confidence (as the lower t statistics for the coefficients tended to signal in advance). However, the tobacco industry has presented something of a challenge throughout this study, and even a weak result can be accepted gratefully.

But now, we do have something rather striking to comment on. Here are three different industries (i.e., Industries 20, 21, and 29), in which significant seasonal variation in the relation of H_t to S_t has been observed. In each case there has been a pattern of *buildup of stocks related to anticipated demand in coming months.*

The reason for the seasonal variation in the three cases are quite different.

1. In the tobacco industry, inventory buildup in nine months of the year is required to support sales in July and December when production (for whatever reason) is lower.

   The theoretical purist may at this point say, "Hold on. It's also possible that the lower production levels in July and December are needed (each year) to enable reduction of the unexpected buildup of inventory during the rest of the year." The objection is a plausible one, though to support it asks that the manufacturers in the industry show both considerable stubbornness to change in pattern, and marked inability to learn in the face of a multiply repeated error.

2. For the food industry, the hypothesis that higher production at the end of the growing season is required to provide inventory needed during the colder months does not seem unreasonable. The alternative hypothesis that lower production was needed to reduce inventories exuberantly (and mistakenly) overstocked during the same period each year is not entirely convincing.

   We are able to observe that production exceeded sales in all eighteen years tested for the months of August and September, and in seventeen of the years for October. For each of the former months, the probability of such an outcome due solely to chance (i.e., deciding on the flip of a coin whether to build inventory or not) would be in the order of 1 in 262,000, and for the latter month, the slightly less unlikely probability of roughly 69 times out of 100,000. At the very least, we can confidently reject the thought that a coin was the decision instrument.

3. For the petroleum industry, the repetitive pattern of building inventory from May through November would seem tacit confirmation of the common belief that fuel bills are higher in the cold months.

   During the eighteen years tested, production exceeded sales sixteen times, in each of the months: July, August, September, and October. In addition, one month in each of the eighteen Septembers and Octobers saw a zero result (i.e., production and sales just equal). The probability, for each month, of such an outcome for reasons ascribed to chance would be 1.167 out of 1,000 for sixteen (+) months, and 1.87 out of 100 in the latter two months, if we count them as only fifteen (+) months. Probably, we can accept the performance as reasonable confirmation that manufacturers in the petroleum industry appear to do a good job of sales prediction.

   However, where does this leave the notion of buffer stocks (i.e., "inventories are carried to provide a cushion against unexpected changes in demand")? The question will be further addressed in the final section of the chapter.

   Here we can reconsider a question raised earlier on the consistency of seasonal patterns. Table 32 shows the number of months (out of eighteen possibilities) in which DS was negative in a given month (i.e., representing a down-turn in sales) for each industry. It does not show whether manufacturers reacted by reducing production, though that answer can be inferred from figures 5 and 6. What table 32 does show is simply how consistently seasonal demand for the industry's products is up or down at various parts of the year. The footnotes at the bottom of the table serve to indicate months in which the historic pattern may have (or be) changed.

   If sales were down(up) in a given month on a purely stochastic basis, we could expect a table in which sixes through twelves predominated, sprinkled with a few larger and smaller numbers. The statistically *unlikely* outcomes would be:

Event	Probability
0 or 18	3.8×10^{-6}
3 or 17	6.5×10^{-5}
2 or 16	1.04×10^{-3}
3 or 15	1.56×10^{-2}

Table 32.   Monthly Upturns and Downturns in Sales for Industries Producing to Stock, as Shown by the Number of Declines in Sales over an Eighteen-Year Period (1959-1976)

Month	Industry Number			
	20	21	28	29
January	12	15	0	12
February	0	3	0	4
March	7	3	0	16
April	13	8	1	3
May	9	3	14	8
June	0	2	13[b]	0
July	17	17	18	14[c]
August	0	3	0	1
September	0	11	0	6
October	10	13[a]	18	9
November	16	4	18	7
December	15	12	18	6

[a] In the last four years, DS was positive.

[b] In the last five years, DS was positive.

[c] In the last three years, DS was positive.

The petroleum industry, somewhat surprisingly, appears to have a less pronounced pattern of seasonal changes in demand than one, a priori, might have expected. However, *very* close examination of the underlying data suggests that in given years, the pattern over a few months' span tends to "slide" one way or another (e.g., that is if we are lucky enough to have a warm January—look out; don't count on a warm February). The close correlation between sales and production in the industry is the more remarkable, given the lack of clearly marked seasonal pattern.

On the other hand, between what Mark Twain had to say about tobacco, and commonly held opinions about the regularity of food intake habits, it is not surprising to find the regularity of sales down(up) turns in Industries 20 and 21 is sufficient to result in seven of the twelve months in each industry being seasonally predictable at a 1 percent level of confidence (two-tailed test) (i.e., the frequency of occurrence being more than chance alone would suggest).

But it is the chemical industry that most notably demonstrates seasonal patterns. Ten of twelve months' regularity in down(up) turn can be considered statistically significant. Of the other two, one represents only fourteen months (where fifteen or more would be needed for significance); and, for the twelfth month, the pattern was one of a decrease in sales for thirteen of fourteen years, but then, what may well be a different pattern began. Since 1972 sales have turned down each year in June, for five years in succession. So, June is still a predictable month—but the call has changed.

Seasonal Behavior of Industries Producing to both Order and Stock

A similar approach can be undertaken toward inspection of the seasonal behavior of industries producing both to order and to stock. However, the previously encountered inability to accurately differentiate between the two functions limits analysis to a verbal description of general characteristics. Because of this limitation, we have arbitrarily chosen a particular industry to serve as the vehicle for discussion.

Table 33 shows the mean monthly values of production, sales, new orders, finished goods inventories, and unfilled orders (i.e., $\bar{P}_t$, $\bar{S}_t$, $\bar{N}_t$, $\bar{H}_t$, and $\bar{U}_t$), and their changes from the month preceding (i.e., DP, DS, DN, DH, and DU) for each calendar month over the 1959–1976 period for Industry 34 (fabricated metals). Figure 7 graphically portrays the mean monthly values of P_t, S_t, N_t, H_t, and U_t.

Sales and production track each other closely, as is the case for industries producing only to stock. This is even more to be expected in the present case, since, by definition, sales to order follow immediately upon production, whereas production to stock is intended to accumulate (or replenish) finished goods inventories from which sales will be (or have been) made. New orders follow a similar track, but interestingly, they regularly exceed both sales and production during the first nine months of the year, and are either lower or roughly coincident with sales and production in the final quarter. From the standpoint of causation or motivation, however, it needs be made clear that sales and production *follow* the receipt of new orders, which "cause them to happen."

The seasonal profile of activity for orders, production, and sales shows twin peaks in June and September, with lower levels at year's end and beginning, plus a bottom in July. Why a peak in June followed by a low level in July? Those familiar with this industry (and ones of similar behavior, e.g.,

Table 33. Seasonal Pattern of Industry 34 as Shown by Inter-Month
Comparison of Production, Sales, New Orders, Finished Goods, Unfilled
Orders, and their Average Monthly Changes (1959-1976)

	1	2	3	4	5	6	7	8	9	10	11	12	(1)
$\overline{P}_t$	3,182	3,488	3,564	3,627	3,633	3,803	3,299	3,639	3,789	3,800	3,620	3,563	3,432
$\overline{S}_t$	3,135	3,436	3,530	3,589	3,609	3,797	3,359	3,664	3,807	3,797	3,597	3,501	3,382
$\overline{N}_t$	3,272	3,549	3,631	3,663	3,666	3,967	3,465	3,760	3,986	3,806	3,567	3,510	3,525
$\overline{H}_t$	1,886	1,938	1,971	2,009	2,034	2,039	1,979	1,955	1,937	1,940	1,963	2,025	2,075
$\overline{U}_t$	12,102	12,215	12,316	12,391	12,448	12,617	12,723	12,819	12,998	13,007	12,978	12,986	13,129
$\overline{DP}$	-104	306	75	63	6	170	-504	445	150	11	-180	-58	-130
$\overline{DS}$	-97	301	94	59	20	188	-438	305	144	-11	-200	-96	-119
$\overline{DN}$	29	277	82	32	3	301	-502	295	226	-180	-239	-57	15
$\overline{DH}$	47	52	34	38	25	6	-60	-25	-18	3	23	62	50
$\overline{DU}$	137	113	101	74	57	170	106	96	179	9	-30	9	143

NOTE: Values expressed in $, $\overline{M}$.

Figure 7.   Mean Monthly Values of Production, Sales,
New Orders, Finished Goods, and Unfilled
Orders ($, $\bar{M}$) for Industry 34 (1959-1976)

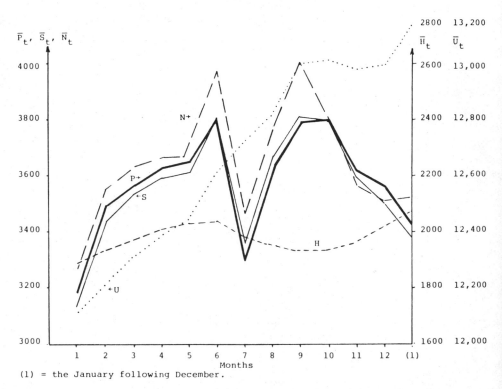

(1) = the January following December.

Industries 35 and 36) point to the pattern prevalent in these industries of closing the plant (or "mill," as it is often called) for one or two weeks in July for the combined purposes of employee vacations and routine maintenance. The sales/production peak in June is then explainable as necessary to accommodate the shutdown period. Without July shutdowns, and a pattern of more continuous activity through the summer months, it is not unreasonable to think that production/sales/order activity would "hump" annually in September or October.

The actual seasonal pattern's regularity is illustrated by the list below, which shows the number of times over the eighteen-year test period for which sales in any month have declined from the month previous level. Eight of the months are sufficiently consistent in direction (i.e., higher, or lower sales volume), that the occurrence cannot be ascribed to chance alone, at a 1 percent level of significance. It is only in the "swing months" of March-May and October in which more random behavior is shown.

Month	Number of Sales Declines
January	16
February	0
March	4
April	5
May	8
June	0
July	18
August	0
September	1
October	9
November	17
December	15

In addition table 33 and figure 7 show a regular pattern of accumulation of finished goods inventories through June, a period of depletion during the third quarter (July-September), and then steady buildup again until the following June. Accumulation of unfilled orders, on the other hand, proceeds in something approaching linear fashion through September (which is the month in which finished goods inventories are at their low point). Then, through the end of the year, while inventories are replenished, there is essentially no further increase in back-logged orders.

This offset in timing, of course, indicates something significant about the nature of the profit-maximizing decision for the production to order, and the production to stock functions within the industry. It appears that firms have regularly decided to produce less to stock than is required to fill incoming orders (i.e., to deplete inventories) during July—September. Then, for the remainder of the year, in the face of a declining rate of receipt of new orders, they regularly produce at a rate which holds unfilled orders more or less constant, while building finished goods inventories. After the beginning of the year, both sales and production increase monthly, following the increase in new orders, and both unfilled orders, and inventories of finished goods through June—when the cycle is repeated.

Obviously, differences in timing and rate of the accumulation/ decumulation of unfilled orders and inventories is central to meaningful analysis. Here the problem arises that we are unable to quantitatively distinguish between the production to order, and the production to stock functions.

At this point, our analysis is unfortunately halted. The choice of Industry 34 for examination, of course, was to illustrate the problem. The dilemma is the same for the other industries producing both to stock and to order— without means of separately identifying sales from stock and sales to order, quantitative analysis eludes us, and only qualitative inferences can be made.

A Production Cycle Inventory Thesis

We have examined a respectable amount of data relating to finished goods inventories, of sales of industries, and of decisions on production levels. A recapitulation is in order of the purposes served (or which have been inferred to be served) by inventories of finished goods held in support of sales from inventory.

One of the better rundowns is provided by Evans:[8]

1. *The transactions motive* is one derived, from the Keynesian motive of similar name for holding money, or, "the amount held for the needs of daily economic activity."

2. *The speculative motive.* "The price of goods held in inventory may be expected to rise, which will result in capital gains, or, manufacturers may hold finished goods in order to circumvent shortages of raw materials."

3. *Buffer stocks.* "Many times firms will incorrectly forecast sales in the coming time period. In these cases it is likely that sales and inventory investment will move in opposite directions. If sales estimates are too low, extra sales will result in depleted inventories. Conversely, if sales estimates are too high, unintended inventories will accumulate."

To this group, it is appropriate to add one other:[9]

4. *Production smoothing.* Adjustment of production *now,* in anticipation of approaching higher (lower) sales, in such a way that larger adjustment of production *later* will be minimized. The idea relates particularly to modifying seasonal/cyclical swings in production level.

Of the four possibilities, the most frequently encountered explanation of inventory behavior is (3). The first three motives are derived from various roots in economic theory. The fourth is basically a practical observation, though from a theoretical standpoint, we recall it has been demonstrated by Vernon Smith that the costs of production increase when output is variable.[10]

The question now to be addressed is, "Which of these motives provides the best explanation for the holding of inventories of finished goods?"

The tobacco industry (Industry 21) behavior of building inventory in anticipation of planned decreases in production does not relate to production smoothing, certainly. (It might more accurately be called "sales smoothing"). In any case, as shown earlier (pp. 000-00), none of the four production to stock industries included in this study demonstrate production smoothing.

It could be argued that the higher production rate of the food industry (Industry 20) in the fall relates to the speculative motive of "holding finished goods to circumvent shortages of raw materials," and perhaps to the transactions motive as well—for after all "you've got to have the goods, to sell them." While we can agree with these statements, as far as they go, they do seem to offer a characterization of behavior more than *an explanation*.

And we have yet to encounter a good example representative of the buffer motive, in spite of the frequency with which it is cited. The essence of the buffer motive explanation is that sales are incorrectly forecasted, and yet, the bulk of the evidence so far examined for industries producing to stock would point to very close estimation by manufacturers of the sales volume of the forthcoming period. An explanation, to be really useful, in other words, must show why inventories of finished goods are useful for manufacturers able to closely estimate next month's sales. The model developed below copes with precisely this point.

We start with the observation that many products are produced on production lines which also produce other products. (We will not here go into joint production theory, which does not directly relate to our present problems.) We observe, also, that commonly, models of production and inventory present the assumption that "one homogeneous product" is made. This, of course, is where the problem starts, for *commonly, is not the "common" case* multiple products, sequentially produced, are closer to the general case. Were it not so, we would not have "change-over" and "set-up" costs to frequently observe; nor would we have companies whose host of products far outnumbers their production facilities.

Consider a process line on which any one of ten products are made. From an operations research approach, the appropriate sequence of products in manufacture, and the economic lot sizes for each product have been determined.[11] One can then project the length of time an entire *production cycle* will require, N days. At this point, we have:

P_i = the ith product, $P_1 - P_{10}$.

q_i = the economic lot size for P_i.

n_i = length of time (days) to produce q_i.

N = length of the entire production cycle; $N = \epsilon n_i$.

Q = volume of all products produced in one cycle;

$Q = \epsilon q_i$.

We assume that P_i will be produced only each cycle,[12] and therefore it is obvious that we hope q_i will equal N days anticipated demand. The obvious question, of course, is "why should anticipated sales even approximate the economic lot size?" The answer is simply that anticipated sales are one of the key determinants of economic lot size.[13]

This brings us to the nub of the matter—what will sales be for the N day period? The answer, of course, is S_i, with the reservation that S_i is not yet available data. We do have available an estimate of S_i, which is $\hat{S}_i$, and there are data at hand on last period's sales, $S_{-1,i}$.

At the end of the current production run of P_i, the finished goods inventory of this product will be:

$$H_i = a_i + q_i \quad^{14}$$
(7.18)

where a_i is the desired level of a buffer stock necessitated by the stochastic nature of sales. It is tempting to sum up all the H_i's to determine the overall finished goods inventory, but the H_i's aren't directly additive on this basis, of course, because of timing differences. Sales have begun on the product which preceded P_i in manufacture, and stocks are almost depleted of the product which follows P_i in the schedule.

The last paragraph does not mean that we do not know what is in current inventory—we do. It is simply:

$$H = a + \epsilon(q_i - SD_i)$$
(7.19)

where $a = \epsilon a_i$, and SD_i is available data showing *sales* to *date*.

Eventually, we reach the point in time at which $SD_i = S_{-1,i}$. The N day period is over.

How well did $\hat{S}_i$ anticipate the result? We do not need to retrieve the notes of our last scheduling meeting—the answer is in our current inventory figures. If $H_i < a_i$, actually realized sales have exceeded our estimate by $(a_i - H_i)$; and, of course, if $H_i > a_i$, sales were below expectations. In either case, q_i for the forthcoming period will require the correction appropriate, and the mill wheels continue to grind.

Our objective is accomplished at this point, but clearly some explanation is needed.

1. We have walked through the decision process and see that it is inherently a *production decision* process, which in turn affects inventory investment.[15]

2. The finished goods inventory for a particular firm (or segment thereof) has been pictured (equation 7.19) as comprised of a safety stock or buffer portion, "a", and the component, $\epsilon(q_i - SD_i)$, which represents goods made in anticipation of near term sales needs less the current sales of each product since its appearance in the production schedule. For the products outlined above, the overall inventory of finished goods can be estimated at any point in time as:

$$H_t \sim a + Q/2$$
(7.20)

3. Individual firms, of course, know the proportion of their finished goods inventories held for near term anticipated sales and for buffer purposes. The information is not normally disseminated beyond the firm, however, and no such data is available for industries in the aggregate.

4. Can the relative sizes of the "a" and "Q/2" segments be estimated in the aggregate, nevertheless? In a word, no.

   However, as our earlier analysis on the subject has demonstrated, the handling of finished goods inventories by industries producing to stock does not support the buffer (or production smoothing) premise, and does point to adjustment of production as the primary means of adjustment to changes in level of sales. Consequently, we can reasonably conclude that the finished goods inventories of industries producing to stock are used in a working/rotating manner in which the "Q/2" portion represents the predominant segment—i.e., $Q/2 > a$, and the bulk of H_t is held for anticipated sales needs, and not because of uncertainty.

5. The mistaken notion that finished goods inventories are primarily buffers probably has arisen because of the prevalence of "one product" models. For these, the need for q_i's has been eliminated by the one product assumption, and all that is left is "a."

8

Financial Factors

So far, the analytical approach of this study has chiefly revolved about the microtheoretic based profit-maximizing models developed in chapters 3 and 4. However, at several points, the importance of financial factors has been found to deserve attention. And, an earlier comment of Louis de Alessi,[1] with respect to adjustment of a firm to change in market conditions, bears repetition. "As Alchian and others have emphasized, however, the crucial concept is the *wealth* effect of the alternative strategies considered by the firm." The subject matter of this chapter is the role of wealth, of financial, factors in the behavior of the firm.

The question being addressed here is not of the "correctness" of the standard microtheory treatment as much as its "completeness." For instance, profit-maximizing behavior is the cornerstone of the theory of the firm—but what is a profit? From a flow standpoint, profit equals revenues minus costs. From a stock standpoint, profit shows up as a change in wealth over the period. Both are correct, but commonly the latter has not been considered.

It is consideration of the firm's behavior from the "stock" or balance sheet perspective that is the purpose (for completeness) of this chapter.

The Firm's Balance Sheet

Given the lack of emphasis normally placed, a brief review of terminology and concepts encompassed here might not be amiss.

The balance sheet is a snapshot which shows, at a particular point in time, the assets held by the firm, what is owed, and the difference between these which represents net worth, or the equity of the shareowners. A very simple example is given below.

The Balance Sheet of SIMPLEFIRM,
in $, as of 7/31/80

Assets			Liabilities and Equity	
(1) Cash	100	(6)	Short-Term Debt	75
(2) Receivables (A/R)	150	(7)	Payables (A/P)	100

(3)	Inventories	200	(8)	Accruals	50
(4)	Total Current Assets	450	(9)	Total Current Liabilities	225
(5)	Fixed Assets (net		(10)	Long-Term Debt	250
	of depreciation)	300			
			(11)	Equity	275
(12)	Total Assets	750	(13)	Total, Liabilities and Equity	750

The assets are the "tools" the firm uses in its business. It has current assets constantly being turned over, and fixed assets which include plant and equipment.

1. Cash signifies the size of checking deposits and liquid assets, such as C.D.'s (and not nickels, dimes, and dollar bills in the main).

2. Receivables are the amounts owed to the firm by customers who have bought on credit (as is prevailing practice).

3. Inventories are familiar ground, but here in the financial sector, the emphasis is on the dollar investment represented rather than the (real) units held.

4. The sum of these, (1) + (2) + (3), is the total of current assets, (4).

5. Fixed assets + (4) = total assets, (12). And now the question is "from where did the funds come which provided these assets?"

6. Some funds have been borrowed from banks.

7. Part of the inventories held have not yet been paid for—payables represent what the firm owes to its suppliers.

8. Accruals represent what the firm owed on 7/31/80, but had not yet paid to recipients normally paid on some set schedule—e.g., wages for workers and tax payments.

9. The sum of these, (6) + (7) + (8) = (9), are the total of current liabilities, and the difference, (4) – (9), represents the firm's "net current" or *working capital* position.

   It is intuitively evident that if working capital were negative, the firm would have a *liquidity problem*. In fact, unless:

$$(1) + (2) - (9) > 0, \qquad (8.1)$$

which represents the "quick" or "acid" test (of a firm's ability to pay those it currently owes in prompt fashion), the firm may be in a liquidity bind, and unable to pay workers and suppliers—or even to borrow short-term funds needed, because of bankers' predilections to avoid slow-pays and no-pays. The merit of the "quick" test is that it points out that the firm cannot count on rapid conversion of inventory into dollars, just as John Stuart Mill's example illustrated earlier.

This example, better than anything else, demonstrates why performance in *both* the real and financial sectors is required for good corporate health.

10. Longer term borrowings represent an important source of funds used by firms to acquire assets. The sum of (9) + (10) shows the total debt of the firm.

11. Equity is on the right hand side of the balance sheet because it also represents an important source of funds—both from the original sale of stock, and of retained profits, which (for the healthy firm) have built up over the years. It is equity, or net worth, which is increased by profits, and diminished by losses.

Arithmetically, $(12) - (9) - (10) = (11)$. And, it should be emphasized that there is *no* box full of hundred dollar bills safely hidden somewhere, with a label upon it saying "retained earnings." *All* previous earnings not earlier disbursed as dividends to shareholders have been converted into assets used by the firm.

The relation between the financial entity, and the firm's flow, or "operating," performance can be shown diagrammatically. In figure 8, the balance sheet elements (or, at least, as many as artistically useful) are shown in boxes with their connecting flows. A particularly useful point of the diagram is that it shows the manufacturing process as repetitive and continuing in nature.

Overmuch should not be made of some of the details of the figure. It suggests, for example, that profits are either disbursed as dividends, or invested in fixed assets—this is true enough, but is not intended to exclude investment of retained earnings into current assets. And, the figure does not suggest, as well as it might, the revolving or "working" nature of the current assets. *All* raw materials (except those wasted or lost) are converted to finished goods inventories. All the latter (save those destroyed or lost) become converted upon sale into payments owed the firm by its customers. And, all accounts receivable (with the usual exception), become converted in turn to CASH, through which "box" all payments must be made.

However, what the figure *does* do is to emphasize the interrelation of the stocks and flows, of the financial entity and the activities in which it engages.

Figure 8.   The Manufacturing Process

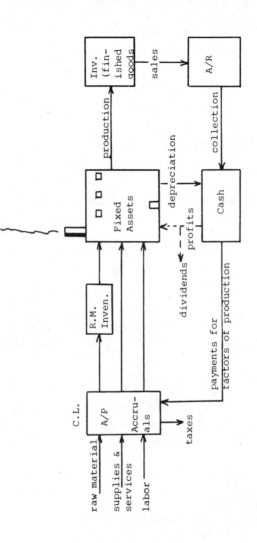

The Financial Data

To study financial performance, "appropriate" data are needed. The financial data on firms and/or industries (i.e., in distinction to that for the whole economy) available to researchers is summarized below:

1. Published information: quarterly and annual reports of corporations, and 10-k's filed with the SEC. In some cases data are available from direct contact with firms and industry associations. Proprietary data series such as "Compustat" are also available.

2. Various NBER series on particular topics, such as: price indices, depreciation, profits, tax payments, wages and salaries, capacity utilization. Balance sheet items are largely not included.

3. The "Quarterly Financial Report on Manufacturing Industries," which is published by the Division of Financial Statistics, FTC. The data used are collected on a sample basis by IRS. The series cover balance sheet and operating income data for two-digit industries (more or less).

The latter source has been utilized for this study. The series do have a few idiosyncracies which should be appreciated, however, because the data while useful, even valuable, are not impeccable, nor entirely consistent with BuCensus statistics. The chief characteristics of the QFR series are:

1. The data have been built up on a statistical sample basis, from corporate income tax returns. One of its main objectives is to provide a cross-sectional view of the performance and financial characteristics of firms of different sizes.

2. Consequently great stress is placed in the makeup of the sample on proper weighting of firms of different sizes. So much stress, in fact, that frequent changes have been made in the sample population. Whenever a sample change has occurred, the QFR reports data on both the old and new basis so that users "may splice" their data appropriately.

   The result, however, for time series study, is that the data are statistically "dirty."

3. The data are segregated as collected by the IRS according to the EI (employer's identification number). This *may* result in better segregation of data by appropriate industry. For instance, General Electric produces, in different divisions, chemicals and jet aircraft engines, as well as electrical products. To the extent that divisions of companies are separately identified by EI, this is helpful.

BuCensus is generally believed to be qualitatively less careful in making these distinctions from the corporate data. However, which is "really better" is not as significant as the simple fact they differ.

4. On the other hand, the QFR has the undesirable characteristic that the data include consolidated results of foreign subsidiaries.

As a result the FTC data do not directly compare with the BuCensus data on such basics as the volume of quarterly production, or the size of inventories held at the end of a quarter. The size of the gap between the quarterly sales reported by QFR vs. those of the BuCensus varies from industry to industry, with the discrepancy largest in the case of the petroleum industry. There, QFR sales are almost double those reported by BuCensus—probably a result of inclusion of foreign subsidiaries' results in the QFR series. Table 34 shows the comparison of SALES (QFR) vs. S_t (BuCensus) for each of the industries in this study.

While the coefficients of the test relation

$$\text{SALES} = a \cdot S_t + u, \tag{8.2}$$

vary more than one might have expected a priori, the t statistics indicate the proportional differences to be clearly delineated, and the good R^2 (in all but the case of the tobacco industry) indicate good fits.

To reduce the differences between the two sets of data, the approach has been used of converting the QFR data on balance sheet and operating income items to a *ratio* with SALES (QFR), and then multiplying the ratio by the BuCensus sales (S_t) figure. For final inventories, INV, from the QFR series, the relation would be:

$$\text{INV} = (\text{INV}_r/\text{SALES}) \times S_t \tag{8.3}$$

where INV_r = the "raw" QFR figure. This approach has two advantages:

1. The new INV figure now represents the same ratio of inventory to BuCensus reported sales, S_t, that the original "raw" figure had to SALES (QFR). In other words, we have preserved the ratio, but have changed the scale of the figure to one which is more consistent in size to data used earlier, such as unfilled orders, for example.

2. The conversion of the QFR series to ratio form smoothes out the "bumps" in the data caused by the discontinuities in the QFR sample base.

Table 34. Regression Test Results of a Comparison of Quarterly Sales Data from QFR and BuCensus for Nine Manufacturing Industries (1958-1976)

Ind.	Coef.	Standard Error	$\underline{t}$ Stat.	$\overline{R}^2$	($, $\overline{M}$)	
					Mean of Dep. Var.	Std. Error of Regr.
20	.973	(.0066)	146	.9772	23,370	1498
21	1.483	(.0331)	45	.6311	1,962	392
28	1.085	(.0127)	85	.9380	13,166	1455
29	1.959	(.0440)	45	.8394	15,391	3337
26	.805	(.0051)	158	.9780	4,964	293
27	.867	(.0187)	46	.8652	4,810	1018
34	.831	(.0080)	103	.9625	8,523	787
35	1.019	(.0078)	131	.9770	13,505	990
36	1.323	(.0144)	92	.9404	13,844	1402

NOTE: SALES = QFR data for sales; S_t = BuCensus data for sales.

Table 35 shows the relation between the "new INV" figure and total inventory, TI, from the BuCensus data from an OLSQ regression test of:

$$INV = b \cdot TI + u' \tag{8.4}$$

The coefficients still "scatter" an appreciable amount, but overall less than was the case in the first table. The t statistics and R^2 measures have been improved by the "ratio treatment," and the standard errors of the regression are proportionally smaller.

From here on, any "QFR" data presented in the discussion will have been transformed on the basis described above.

Working Capital Structure

Figure 8, and the accompanying discussion, emphasized the relation between financial stocks and operating flows. It suggests the possibility of constructing

Table 35.　Regression Test Results of a Comparison of Quarterly Inventory Data from QRF and BuCensus for Nine Manufacturing Industries (1958-1976)

Ind.	Coef.	Standard Error	t Stat.	$\bar{R}^2$	($, \bar{M}$) Mean of Dep. Var.	($, \bar{M}$) Std. Error of Regr.
20	1.338	(.0060)	223	.9874	11,128	460
21	.910	(.0128)	71	.7328	2,156	268
28	1.303	(.0090)	145	.9792	7;749	507
29	1.089	(.0083)	131	.9622	2,556	178
26	1.223	(.0105)	116	.9571	3,140	249
27	1.037	(.0163)	64	.7682	2,175	305
34	1.034	(.0075)	138	.9688	7,519	501
35	.965	(.0062)	155	.9819	11,787	719
36	1.135	(.0052)	220	.9898	8,989	383

NOTE:　$INV = INV_{(QFR)} \cdot \dfrac{S_t}{SALES}$, INV = QFR reported total inventories where: S_t = BuCensus sales for the period, and SALES = QFR reported sales; TI = BuCensus data for total inventories.

a "financial stocks" model. An appropriate starting point would be to turn equation (4.1) around, which would yield:

$$DH_t = P_t^s - S_t^s, \tag{8.5}$$

and we see that the change in finished goods inventories is the resultant of two flows: (1) an inflow of P_t^s which is itself an outflow from raw material inventory (or in some cases, from WIP); (2) and an outflow of S_t^s, which in turn is an inflow into Receivables (i.e., the total amount owed the firm by its customers at any time).

And, we can observe the change in accounts receivable as:

$$DR_t = S_t - C_t, \tag{8.6}$$

which shows: (1) an inflow, S_t, itself the sum of outflows from H_t (for S_t^s) and from U_t (for S_t^o); and (2) an outflow representing customer's payments, C_t, collected during the period.

The flows into and out of CASH are more complicated. The inflows are: (1) the collections, C_t (a portion of which will later turn out to be depreciation); (2) from short-term borrowings; and (3) from changes in the firm's capital structure (e.g., sales of additional stock, sale of bonds, etc.).

The outflows represent every payment of any kind by the firm, which makes CASH a sort of "communications center." Outflows include: (4) payments for goods and services purchased (through accounts payable); (5) wages and taxes (through accruals); and (6) repayment of short-term borrowings and interest.

We can assume the firm keeps close track of its costs of production (one of which is depreciation), its sales revenues, and the difference which represents its operating profits. After taxes have been paid, there are additional outflows from CASH: (7) dividends are paid to shareholders—normally representing only part of profits; (8) and the remainder (of profits) goes into acquisition of new assets, or perhaps in improving the firm's net worth by reducing debt (technically, through the surplus account); (9) and finally, the pleasant discovery is made that there is a little more cash on hand than so far figured. Aha! The extra amount precisely equals depreciation (which is why the alert accountant has already figured depreciation as part of the cash flow). Its disposition, or outflow, is precisely the same as for (8).

The traffic management of these cash flows is less complicated than it looks, because of two helpful rules:

1. It takes cash to increase the firm's assets (e.g., to buy a typewriter) or to decrease liabilities (e.g., to pay a bill which is due).

2. It generates cash to reduce an asset (e.g., sell something) or to increase a liability (e.g., to borrow).

And the *two vital rules* on cash management are:

1. *Don't have too little*—or, it is terribly expensive. If the firm is unable to pay its bills on time, to pay interest and principal amounts due on loans, to meet its payrolls, etc., resultant disruptions to the orderly conduct of its business can represent very large opportunity costs.

2. *Don't have too much*—it can be very, very expensive (again in the opportunity cost sense) to forego having the surplus liquid funds not properly working and turning over. To illustrate the point, liquid funds

truly in excess of the amount needed could be usefully used to repay debt, thereby reducing the costs of debt service.

If there are extra costs to *too low* a CASH level as well as *too high*, we are fairly well assured that somewhere in between there is a minimum cost level to be found. If we follow the Modigliani and Holt[2] approach of approximating the cost structure with a quadratic expression, we would have:

$$C_{cash} = a_1 + b_1 \cdot (CASH) + c_1 \cdot (CASH)^2, \tag{8.7}$$

where: C_{cash} = cost of this capital account over a period.

Similarly, there are obviously extra costs (in the opportunity cost sense) to too low or too high a raw materials inventory (RM). Additional carrying costs if too high a level, and the potential of losses to be incurred if too low an inventory runs out. Or receivables can be:

1. Too high, either by overly lenient credit terms extended to customers, or by lax credit policies which have permitted slow-pays and no-pays to be among purchasers of the firm's products.

2. Too low, because of overly strict credit policies, which discourages interest among would be buyers, and thereby reduces the firm's revenues. (If R is "too low" simply because of poor design or quality of product, the firm faces potential losses or opportunity costs of even greater magnitude.)

Not only can we impute extra costs to each of the current assets when held at too high or too low a level, but the same argument is just as applicable to the current liabilities. For example, payables (PAY) which are too low imply the firm is paying too soon and not taking proper advantage of the free trade credit available to it. Too high a level implies the firm to be a slow payer of bills, thus endangering its supplier relationships—with lurking opportunity costs of shutdowns or slowdowns caused by cut-off or reduction of needed supplies. Hence, we could write:

$$C_{pay} = a_2 + b_2 \cdot PAY + c_2 \cdot (PAY)^2. \tag{8.8}$$

And similarly for each current asset and current liability. And the remainder is in order here that the similar thing was earlier demonstrated (chapter 4) for unfilled orders, as well. A general expression of quadratic cost approximation for any current financial stock would simply be:

$$C_i = a_i + b_i \cdot (Stock_i) + c_i \cdot (Stock_i)^2. \tag{8.9}$$

By differentiating (9.11) with respect to Stock$_i$ we obtain:

$$DC_i/d \; Stock_i = b_i + 2c_i \cdot (Stock), \tag{8.10}$$

and we have assurance of a determinate solution under any given short-run conditions, even though we do not necessarily know the coefficients b_i and c_i (a_i having already left the scene by differentiation).

We may assume the profit-maximizing firm is already reasonably aware of this, and has been diligently at work to determine and establish optimum levels for these various current financial stocks.

Empirical Observations

We should be able to test how well the levels of the various financial stocks have been established and maintained. All that is needed is to test each working capital stock (or its first differences) against the two or more flows appropriate in each case. Unfortunately, we cannot count on the necessary information being readily available. For example: (1) to test H_t or U_t, we should have both P^s and N^s in the first case, and P^o and N^o in the second; (2) to test RM or PAY would require having information on the rates of purchase and use of goods and supplies.

However, if we cannot readily test the level (or changes of the level) of a particular financial stock as our dependent variable in a regression, can we not reverse the process? In effect, we would be assuming that the levels of the various working capital components were actually at cost-minimizing levels, and attempting to verify this by using as the dependent variable of our test, whatever flow variable we can identify as the "most representative" of both the firm's level of business at various points in time *and* of itself representing a profit-maximizing (or close approximation thereof) level of activity—(this is necessarily a short-run model, for the firm's longer term financial stocks are not included).

It would seem that the level of production meets our requirements. First, because most of the factors of cost and profitability are embedded in the production process itself. Second, much (though not all) of the scheme of other flows follow from the level of production (e.g., actual sales to order depend directly on production to order); and separately, in chapter 7, it was demonstrated that production to stock correlates closely with new orders/sales from stock. And finally, we have seen earlier that actual production levels for the industries in the study have shown very good conformance to a profit-maximizing "decision rule." So, while a little backwards about, the approach should serve.

Our immediate object, then, is to test the level of production, for each of the nine industries studied, against components of working capital. These results can be compared with those obtained in previous chapters, where each industry's production level has been "explained" by "real," or flow, variables. The point to be observed is whether the profit-maximizing level of production (as we have previously judged it) is as well explained by financial variables, as by real ones. The tests to be made are outlined in (2) and (3) below, and the earlier results with which these are to be compared are described in (1).

1. First, for reference purposes, the reader will wish to refer to table 3, which showed OLSQ regression results for testing the relation:

$$P_t = d_0 + d_1 \cdot P_{t-1} + d_2 \cdot H_{t-1} + d_3 \cdot N_t + u_t$$

   for Industries 20, 21, 28, and 29.

   Also for reference, table 36 summarizes the results for Equation (4.31), the "decision rule" model production level of industries producing both to stock and order.

Table 36.   A Summary of Regression Results for Industries which Produce to both Stock and Order, using Decision Rule (4.31). BuCensus Quarterly Data, Seasonally Nonadjusted (1958-1976)

$$P_t = n_0 + (n_1 - n_2)DH_{t-1} + n_2 P_{t-1} + n_3 H_{t-1} + n_u U_{t-1} + n_6 N_t + w_t$$

Ind. No.	Mean of Dep. Var.	Std. Error of Regr.	$\bar{R}^2$
26	6,310	234	.9936
27	6,087	60.5	.9994
34	10,906	368	.9941
35	13,847	808	.9873
36	10,935	385	.9920

NOTE: in $, $\bar{M}$.

2. A simple and straightforward relation, as an initial test, would be:

$$P_t = a_1 \cdot CA + a_2 \cdot CL + u_t' , \qquad (8.11)$$

   where CA = current assets, and CL = current liabilities.

It has a built-in disadvantage, however, that events important to firms are not clearly shown by changes in current assets and current liabilities. For example, sale of goods from inventory reduces inventory, and adds an equivalent amount to receivables. Clearly, two otherwise similar firms would find their circumstances very different, if one were selling its product, and the other not. Therefore, we have the question to consider as to whether current financial assets and liabilities can be weighed together, as in (8.11), or whether the individual components of each must be separated, as will be done in the next test.[3]

Results of testing equation (8.11) are shown in table 37. While the test results reported do not show as close a fit as their counterpart regressions described in (1), from either the standpoint of larger standard errors of the regression, or $\bar{R}^2$'s, the results can be considered reasonably satisfactory support of the hypothesis of the test. However, this attempt has essentially been a shortcut (see footnote 3). We have no real reason to think that current assets or current liabilities are substitutable as groups for the individual balance sheet items they comprise (other than the support of the results themselves).

3. The main test results, therefore, are those which next appear. Table 38 shows results from OLSQ regression test of a relation containing the principal (but not all) current account stock financial elements

$$P_t = a_1 \cdot CASH + a_2 \cdot R + a_3 \cdot INV + a_4 \cdot SHLN$$
$$+ a_5 PAY + u'', \tag{8.12}$$

where: R = receivables, INV = total (QFR) inventories, SHLN = short-term borrowings, and PAY = payables.

Overall, and with the exception once again of Industry 21, the testing of financial stocks assumed to be at profit-maximizing levels vs. P_t, approximating the same criterion, gives very good fits for the data and can be considered to confirm the basic thesis—i.e., that the financial stocks are necessary, part and parcel, in the overall firm picture. From the standpoint of the somewhat larger standard errors of regression than shown on table 36 (or on table 3 for the production to stock industries), and of $\bar{R}^2$'s which are lower, except for Industry 35, this testing of financial stocks against the profit-maximizing levels or production yields results not quite as good as those developed in chapters 1 and 4 for operating flows. But the real point is not "which is better?" as much as "do they both belong?"—and to the latter question we can give an affirmative answer.

Looking at table 38 results in detail, we see a sprinkling of negative signs, all but one of which are in the INV and SHLN coefficient columns. In fact, in

Table 37. Regression Results for Nine Industries, with Production Level
Tested against Current Assets and Current Liabilities, QFR and
BuCensus Quarterly Data, Seasonally Nonadjusted (1958-1976)

Ind. No.	Coef. of CA	t stat.	Coef. of CL	t stat.	$\bar{R}^2$	$(\$, \bar{M})$ std. Error of Regr.
20	.814	17.1	.526	5.55	.9875	1070
21	.393	11.9	.263	2.83	.6613	181
28	.354	5.58	.691	4.53	.9824	758
29	.197	2.32	1.203	7.58	.9372	1216
26	.132	3.10	1.527	16.3	.9543	574
27	.231	2.60	1.108	5.61	.9743	351
34	.545	12.9	.260	2.93	.9854	523
35	.031	2.27	1.133	31.8	.9343	1663
36	.698	17.6	-.262	-3.31	.9829	520

NOTE: $P_t = a_1 \cdot CA + a_2 \cdot CL + u'$.

Table 38. Regression Results for Nine Industries, with Production Level Tested against Components of Working Capital, Quarterly QFR and BuCensus Data, Seasonally Nonadjusted (1958-1976)

$$P_t = a_1 \cdot CASH + a_2 REC + a_3 INV + a_4 SHLN + a_5 PAY + u''$$

Ind. No.	Coefficients of Variables					$\bar{R}^2$	Std. Error of Regr.
	CASH	REC	INV	SHLN	PAY		
20	2.125 (7.67)	1.838 (7.36)	-.418 -(1.78)	.139 (.587)	2.090 (6.59)	.9932	802
21	1.803 (2.439)	1.948 (7.33)	.296 (6.70)	-.482 -(2.666)	-.657 -(1.588)	.7530	158
28	.155 (1.051)	.569 (3.918)	.409 (3.175)	-.564 -(1.507)	1.956 (7.00)	.9924	508
29	.921 (10.1)	.230 (1.371)	-.716 -(4.79)	2.62 (6.23)	2.29 (8.26)	.9906	480
26	1.525 (7.80)	.173 (.696)	.174 (.780)	.857 (2.306)	3.21 (6.31)	.9814	374
27	.557 (2.302)	.848 (5.85)	.071 (.307)	-1.325 -(2.044)	1.786 (4.40)	.9760	346
34	.823 (4.57)	1.162 (8.12)	.0074 (.0423)	.389 (1.258)	.706 (1.660)	.9891	464
35	.617 (4.78)	.344 (3.60)	.306 (2.621)	.0783 (.331)	1.377 (4.016)	.9900	663
36	.649 (3.83)	.781 (4.87)	.360 (4.28)	-.252 -(1.36)	.572 (2.65)	.9889	428

NOTE: (t statistics) of coefficients in parentheses, values of standard error of regression in ($\$$, M).

six cases out of nine (and narrowly missing in two more) one or the other *but not both* of the coefficients are negative for these two, strongly indicative of some special relationship between the two—perhaps inverse (but we could expect complementary). The other side of the coin for this same observation is that we have previously seen that RM, WIP, and HT have somewhat different characteristics, and that it may be a source of distortion that in the present test the three are lumped together.

There is always the urge, when one is building models, to add additional explanatory variables (either in this, or any other attractive category)—and this should only be done after close attention has been paid to whether any new regressor has significantly improved the basic explanation. That part of the analysis represents one bridge further than this study has attempted to go.

The other solitary negative sign (for PAY) of table 38 is found, of course, in the tobacco industry. We must guard against the temptation to dismiss elements of unexpected behavior which occur in Industry 21, with a summary comment of, "Of course!" The explanation in this case would seem to lie in the direction indicated by the huge RM inventories held by the tobacco industry (which tend seasonally to be highest when production is seasonally low). The payables represent, of course, the payments to be made for the leaf tobacco, and therefore are apt also to have a seasonal bias, and therefore a poor (or negative) correlation with P_t is not unexpected.

We can conclude that our short-term financial model has been useful in demonstrating the significance of the financial stocks for firms, but that a model which incorporated all flows of funds would be needed for more rigorous use. We will be satisfied here with the simple model's use in showing that the financial stocks of the firm are as much a part of the picture as the flow quantities in explanation of firms' behavior.

Autocorrelation and Collinearity

At several earlier points in this study, note has been made of the possible effects of multicollinearity and serial correlation of errors upon the analysis. Examination of this topic is our final order of business.

The logic of the OLSQ method depends on a number of assumptions. Two important ones are that explanatory variables are not perfectly correlated with each other, and that successive values of the error term are independent of each other. If these assumptions are not satisfied, the consequences are respectively termed multicollinearity and autocorrelation.

Although perfect linear correlation of variables is seldom if ever encountered, the explanatory variables in time series data are generally intercorrelated to some extent, and autocorrelation is regularly suspected (if not always found) in time series regressions. In this section, the regression results obtained from equations (8.11) and (8.12) will be examined for evidence of multicollinearity and/or autocorrelation, the possible effects of either, and how such effects might affect interpretation of results.

Farrar-Glauber Test for Multicollinearity

To begin a description of the Farrar-Glauber test, it is helpful to note that if a pair of explanatory variables are orthogonal (i.e., have no intercorrelation), their correlation coefficient, $r_{x_i x_j} = 0$. The correlation coefficient itself is represented by:

$$r_{x_ix_j} = \frac{\Sigma_{x_ix_j}}{\sqrt{\Sigma x_i^2} \cdot \sqrt{\Sigma x_j^2}} \qquad (8.13)$$

where x_i and x_j are deviations from the mean of the i'th and jth variables. At the other extreme, when the variables are perfectly linearly correlated (i.e., perfectly collinear), $r_{x_ix_j} = 1$.

This might suggest the technique of one-by-one review of the relationship between explanatory variables to see which (nd how many) showed correlation coefficients approximating unity. The Farrar-Glauber test for identification of multicollinearity uses a less cumbersome approach. It is obvious that the matrix of correlation coefficients of the explanatory variables would be of the form:

$$
\begin{array}{ccccc}
1 & r_{x_1x_2} & r_{x_1x_3} & - & r_{x_1x_n} \\
r_{x_2x_1} & 1 & r_{x_2x_3} & - & r_{x_2x_n} \\
r_{x_3x_1} & r_{x_3x_2} & 1 & - & r_{x_3x_n} \\
\cdot & \cdot & \cdot & \cdot & \cdot \\
\cdot & \cdot & \cdot & \cdot & \cdot \\
\cdot & \cdot & \cdot & \cdot & \cdot \\
r_{x_nx_1} & r_{x_nx_2} & r_{x_nx_3} & - & 1
\end{array}
$$

However, with equation (8.13) in mind, the matrix itself can also be viewed as the determinant, in standardized form, of the correlation coefficients of the explanatory variables. Its values would be unity for perfectly othogonal variables, and zero in the case of perfect multicollinearity.

The Farrar and Glauber method for identification of multicollinearity is statistical in nature, and is based on the relation derived by the authors that:

$$*chi^2 = [n - 1 - 1/6(2K + 5)] \cdot \ln \text{ (value of the}$$

$$\text{standardized determinant)} \qquad (8.14)$$

where n = number of time series observations and k = number of explanatory variables. The calculated value ($*chi^2$) has $1/2k$ $(k - 1)$ degrees of freedom.

Farrar and Glauber treat multicollinearity as a departure from orthogonality, using the calculated chi^2 value to test:

H_0 = The X's are orthogonal, i.e., there is zero collinearity; or, $H_0: |X'X| = 1$, where $|X'X|$ represents the standardized determinant of dependent variables.

H_1 = The X's are not orthogonal, i.e., some degree of multicollinearity exists, or $H_1: |X'X| \neq 1$.

The $*chi^2$ value serves two purposes:

1. It can be compared with the theoretical (tabulated) value for the chi^2 distribution at any desired level of significance. A value of the calculated statistic greater than the theoretical value calls for rejection of the null hypothesis, and signifies some degree of collinearity.

2. The higher the value of the calculated statistic, the greater is the departure from orthogonality, and hence, the closer the approach to multicollinearity.

From this, it can be seen that a calculated chi^2 lower than the theoretical value would mean acceptance of the hypothesis of orthogonal variables. However, it would be more in the spirit of the test method to view such a result simply as indicating no significant degree of multicollinearity.

Farrar-Glauber Test Results

In this section, FG (Farrar-Glauber) test results are examined, using Industry 28 as an example. As part of the examination, use will be made of subperiods of the overall 1958–1976 test period, for which regression results were shown earlier (on table 23).

For Equation (8.12) (repeated here for convenience):

$$P_t = a_1 \cdot CASH + a_2 \cdot REC + a_3 \cdot INV + a_4 \cdot SHLN$$
$$+ a_5 \cdot PAY + u,$$

and the FG test results were:

Number of Observations	Value of Determinant	Calculation Chi^2 (10 Degrees of Freedom)	Theoretical Chi^2 at 1% Level of Significance
75	.13376	143.8	23.2

The calculated chi^2 is appreciably larger than the theoretic value at the 1 percent level of significance, and a significant degree of multicollinearity is indicated. It would be possible to continue with the FG approach to determine which variables are involved in the multicollinear relation, but this is not undertaken here.

Equation (8.11) (repeated here) had two explanatory variables:

$$P_t = a_1 \cdot CA + a_2 \cdot CL + u'.$$

It would be evident in this case, from the standardized determinant alone, that significant correlation existed between the two X's:

	X_1	X_2
X_1	1	.99777
X_2	.99777	1

However, to follow through as intended with the FG test results, we have:

Number of Observations	Value of Determinant	Calculation Chi^2 (10 Degrees of Freedom)	Theoretical Chi^2 at 1% Level of Significance
75	.00445	392	6.63

And, a substantial degree of collinearity between the variables, CA and CL, has been confirmed using the Farrar-Glauber method of analysis.

Effects of Multicollinearity

The effects of the multicollinearity observed can be illustrated by inspection of the results shown on tables 39 and 40.[5] These give the regression results obtained with equations (8.11) and (8.12), respectively, when the overall 1958-01 through 1976-04 period is divided into the four consecutive segments earlier used for analysis. These were:

From	To	Period	Number of Observations,
1958-01	1968-04	I	43
1969-01	1970-03	II	7
1970-04	1974-03	III	16
1974-04	1976-04	IV	9

As a group, the results obtained from the regressions of the shorter period (I–IV) also show "good fits." Except for period II (the 1969-01 through 1970-03 segment), which was notable for a rapidly rising inventory ratio, the R^2's obtained for the subperiods are not greatly inferior to the excellent results obtained for the overall (1958–1976) test period in both tables. For the subperiods, the *t* statistics for individual coefficients are sometimes improved, though more frequently not. The standard error of the regression averages about 30 percent less for the four subperiods, than for the test period as a whole.

Table 39. Regression Results for Industry 28, with Production Level Tested against Current Assets and Current Liabilities, QFR and BuCensus Quarterly Data, Nonseasonally Adjusted (for 1958-1976, and Four Subperiods)

Per.	No. of Obs. Util.	For CA			For CL			For Regression			
		Coef.	Std. Error	$\frac{t}{stat.}$	Coef.	Std. Error	$\frac{t}{stat.}$	$\bar{R}^2$	$\$\bar{M}$, Std. Er. of Regr.	D-W stat.
	75	.354	.063	5.58	.691	.152	4.53	.9824	758	.5913
I	43	.589	.043	13.71	.079	.114	.690	.9842	225	2.0576
II	7	1.000	.241	4.16	-.923	.567	-1.63	.5366	239	2.5699
III	16	-.554	.233	-2.37	2.78	.548	5.08	.9389	815	1.2835
IV	9	.700	.231	3.03	-.062	.537	-.012	.8019	818	1.815

Table 40. Regression Results for Industry 28, with Production Level Tested against Components of Working Capital, QFR and BuCensus Quarterly Data, Nonseasonally Adjusted (for 1958-1976, and Four Subperiods)

No. of Obs. Util.		Explanatory Variable					For Regression		
		CASH	REC	INV	SHLN	PAY	$\bar{R}^2$	$\bar{\$M}$, Std. Error of Regr.	D-W Stat.
75	coef.	.155	.569	.409	-.564	1.956	.9924	508	.6774
	std. error	.148	.145	.129	.374	.279			
	t stat.	1.051	3.918	3.175	-1.507	7.000			
43	coef.	.661	.898	.414	.578	.078	.9859	222	2.2207
	std. error	.134	.137	.163	.412	.339			
	t stat.	4.949	6.536	2.541	1.402	.229			
7	coef.	.632	.041	1.133	-1.264	.927	.7218	293	2.707
	std. error	1.04	.774	1.086	3.553	1.184			
	t stat.	.608	.053	1.043	-.356	.782			
16	coef.	-1.472	1.651	.0155	-1.333	1.920	.9920	332	1.820
	std. error	.233	.281	.197	.824	.413			
	t stat.	-6.315	5.880	.276	-.617	4.652			
9	coef.	-.574	1.592	.023	-.323	1.682	.9591	492	1.909
	std. error	.550	.467	.458	.911	.924			
	t stat.	-1.044	3.412	.049	-.453	1.821			

The most significant observation, however, is the considerable variability of individual coefficients in both sign and magnitude. In most cases, the differences are greater than would be expected from the standard errors reported. In other words, there is strong indication that while correlations are good between dependent and explanatory variables, the coefficients have not been determined with precision—and further, that the standard errors seriously understate the matter. In other words, given the presence of strong collinearity between explanatory variables, the OLSQ results have not clearly distinguished between the effects of individual variables, even though overall correlation between explanatory variables (as a group) and dependent variables appears "good."

In demonstration of the latter observation, it could readily be shown that very similar "predicted" values of P_t, the dependent variable, are obtained when actual explanatory data, for any given quarter, are plugged into these widely divergent regression relations. We can conclude that the primary task undertaken (of demonstrating good correlation between explanatory variables and P_t) has been accomplished, but that the regression coefficients obtained through OLSQ regressions do not accurately portray the relationships.

These conclusions are subject to possible criticism from the standpoint of recognized shortcomings of the Farrar-Glauber test. As Judge et al.[6] have put it, "Despite the popular attention this test has received, there are several critical problems associated with it that render it largely useless." These are:

1. The Farrar-Glauber assumption of an approximate chi^2 distribution of the test statistic is derived on the basis of t independent observations drawn from a joint normal distribution of independent and dependent variables. But, "given the nonexperimental nature of economics, it is very likely that samples all contain dependent observations." The observation is appropriate in the case of the present analysis, and therefore, the statistical basis for the chi^2 distribution and the scale for measurement of multicollinearity are undermined.

2. One of the underlying assumptions of classical linear regression is that explanatory variables are not perfectly linearly correlated, i.e., $r_{x_i x_j} \neq 1$. The Farrar-Glauber test, however, is couched in terms of: $H_0: |X'X| = 1$, and $H_1: |X'X| \neq 1$, where $|X'X|$ represents the standardized determinant of the explanatory variables. It is true, of course, that if any pair of $r_{x_i x_j}$ were equal to unity, $|X'X|$ would equal zero, and multicollinearity would exist. And, if $r_{x_i x_j}$ were unity for *each* pair of explanatory variables, $|X'X|$ would still equal zero, and there would be "perfect" multicollinearity. Equally clear-cut is the situation in which the variables are othogonal, i.e., not at all correlated, and $r_{x_i x_j} = 0$ while $|X'X| = 1$.

In the normal case, the relation is apt to lie somewhere between these polar cases. The least utility provided the analyst by the Farrar-Glauber test probably occurs in the range of determinant values wherein the null hypothesis, H_0, is either weakly confirmed or rejected. This leads, for example, to judgments on the existence (or absence) of multicollinearity being affected by sample design.

These critical considerations would pose a definite problem in the case of analyses leading to conclusions either (weakly) rejecting the presence of multicollinearity, or indicative of "some" degree of multicollinearity. However, where the incidence of the problem is as strongly marked as in the preceding analysis, the conclusion reached that a strong degree of multicollinearity does indeed exist (and with the effects shown on values of coefficients) can be viewed as not substantially affected by the problems reviewed above.

Autocorrelation

We turn next to consideration of autocorrelation. In analysis of time series data, if the value of "u" for a particular time period is correlated with its own value for a preceding period, there is serial correlation, or autocorrelation, of the random variable.

A simple case of autocorrelation obtains when there is a linear relationship between any two successive values of "u," i.e., $u_t = \rho\, u_{t-1} + t$, where $\rho =$ the autocorrelation coefficient ($-1 \leq \rho \leq 1$). Where ρ has a positive value, there is *positive* autocorrelation. This implies that a positive value of "u" will likely be followed by another positive "u" in the next period; and similarly, a negative "u" will tend to be followed by another of the same sign. Such a pattern represents a first order autoregressive relationship.

Autocorrelation occurs relatively frequently in economic time series, and examination of the results shown in tables 37 and 38, with this in mind, is appropriate.

The well-known Durbin-Watson test is useful in investigating the presence/absence of first order autocorrelation. The D-W statistic, "d," is defined:

$$d = \frac{\sum_{t-2}^{n} (e_t - e_{t-1})^2}{\sum_{n-1}^{n} (e_t^2)}, \tag{8.15}$$

where $e_t =$ the value of the error term for period t. And, it can be shown that:

$$d \sim 2 \cdot (1 - \hat{\rho}), \tag{8.16}$$

where $\hat{\rho} =$ the estimated value of the autocorrelation coefficient. It follows from this that "d" will have values between 0 and 4. Positive values of ρ (which tend somewhat more frequently to be encountered when autocorrelation exists) are shown by values of $d < 2$; and, of course, when $\rho = 0$, $d = 2$.

The D-W test has, as its null hypothesis: H_0: $\rho = 0$, and the alternate hypothesis: H_1: $\rho \neq 0$. Tables have been prepared for the upper and lower d-statistic values (d_u and d_l, respectively) for the 5 percent and 1 percent levels of significance. The scheme for interpretation of results for a particular test statistic, d^*, is shown below:

For values of $d^* < 2$: (1) For $d^* < d_l$, the null hypothesis is rejected, and positive autocorrelation of the first order is accepted; (2) for $d^* > d_u$, the null hypothesis of no autocorrelation is accepted; (3) if $d_l < d^* < d_u$, the test is inconclusive.

For values of $d^* > 2$: (1) for $d^* > (4 - d_l)$, the null hypothesis is rejected, and negative autocorrelation of the first order is accepted; (2) for $d^* < (4 - d_u)$, the null hypothesis of no autocorrelation is accepted; (3) if $(4 - d_l) > d^* > (4 - d_u)$, the test is inconclusive.

As a practical matter, the relative merits of the test intuitively would seem connected with the frequency with which either results (1) or (2) were signalled. On the other hand, frequent "no decision," (3), results would diminish utility of the test. And, in fact, just to avoid the latter shortcoming, some analysts (conveniently but incorrectly) have adopted a shortcut form of the test which simply ignores d_l, and treats d_u as the decision figure.

Durbin-Watson Test Results

Fortunately, from the standpoint of test interpretation, the test results obtained with the present study are straightforward, and there is no need to utilize the abridged form of the D-W test.

The Durbin-Watson test results from the OLSQ regressions of equations (8.11) and (8.12) were originally tabulated on tables 37 and 38, for the nine industries studied in this paper. In table 41, these D-W results are repeated, *plus* the appropriate interpretation of the test statistic for seventy-five quarterly observations, and the indicated number of variables.

The D-W test statistics are, in most cases, markedly smaller than two, and positive autocorrelation at the 1 percent level of significance for six industries is indicated in each list, plus a seventh at the 5 percent level of significance. The test statistics for Industry 34 were not quite as low, an can best be considered inconclusive. Only in the case of Industry 36 were there test statistics over two, indicating a possible tendency toward negative autocorrelation—but not strongly enough for this assumption to be affirmed.

The similarity of behavior toward well-marked positive autocorrelation for most of these industries suggests that some additional attention to the

Table 41. Durbin-Watson Test Statistics and Interpretation for Nine Industries, from REgression Results on Equations (8.11) and (8.12), QFR and BuCensus Quarterly Data, Nonseasonally Adjusted (1958-1976)

Ind.	d*	For Eq. (8.11) (2 variables) Interpretation	d*	For Eq. (8.12) (5 variables) Interpretation
20	1.1243	positive autocorrelation @ 1%	.8011	positive autocorrelation @ 1%
21	.5823	positive autocorrelation @ 1%	.7651	positive autocorrelation @ 1%
28	.5913	positive autocorrelation @ 1%	.6774	positive autocorrelation @ 1%
29	.4600	positive autocorrelation @ 1%	1.4138	positive autocor. @ 5%; inconclusive @ 1%
26	.5846	positive autocorrelation @ 1%	.7664	positive autocorrelation @ 1%
27	1.2697	positive autocorrelation @ 1%	.9756	positive autocorrelation @ 1%
34	1.5744	no autocor. @ 1%; inconclusive @ 5%	1.7414	no autocor. @ 1%; inconclusive @ 5%
35	1.4848	positive autocorrelation @ 5% (inconclusive @ 1%)	1.0314	positive autocorrelation @ 1%
36	2.1331	no autocorrelation @ 1% (or 5%)	2.4303	inconclusive @ 1% and 5%

NOTE: Eq. (8.11): $P_t = a_1 \cdot CA + a_2 \cdot CL + u'_t$; Eq. (8.12): $P_t = a_1 \cdot CASH + a_2 \cdot R + a_3 \cdot INV + a_4 \cdot SHLN + a_5 PAY + u''$.

subject is in order, starting with the consequences in OLSQ regressions, when there is temporal dependence of the error term.

As summarized by Koutsoyiannis,[7] these are:

1. While the values of parameter estimates are statistically unbiased, the estimates are not best (in the BLUE sense).

2. Autocorrelation in the error term is frequently accompanied by autocorrelation of the explanatory variables themselves.

3. Particularly in the case of (2), the variance both of the error term and of the parameter estimates may be seriously underestimated.

Two approaches have been undertaken below for closer examination of the problem. For this purpose, results from one particular industry will be subjected to more detailed scrutiny. Industry 28 is a logical choice, with its clearly marked pattern of positive autocorrelation.

1. The first approach involves examination of results obtained when the overall period of study is broken into the shorter segments utilized a few pages earlier.

2. Use of the Cochrane-Orcutt iterative technique to estimate the value of the correlation coefficient, ρ, and also to obtain regression results for which the original (i.e., actual) data have been transformed to a "corrected" data set by application of the estimated correlation coefficient.

Durbin-Watson Test Results with Shorter Time Periods: Industry 28

The reminder may be helpful here that the four subdivison of the overall (1958-01 through 1976-04) test period do not represent four periods of equal length, but rather periods in which the behavior of the inventory ratio (H_t / S_t) differed from the period previous, as outlined below:

Period	Number of Quarters	H_t / S_t Behavior
I	43	level
II	7	increasing
III	16	decreasing
IV	9	level (but lower than 1)

The OLSQ regression results presented earlier (tables 39 and 40) included the D-W test statistics for both the overall test period and its subdivisions for equation (8.11) (two variables) and for equation (8.12) (five variables), for

Industry 28. For comparative purposes, values of $\hat{\rho}$ are listed below, as derived from the approximate relation: $\hat{\rho} \sim 1 - \dfrac{d^*}{2}$ (from equation 8.16):

Period	Number of Quarterly Observations	$\hat{\rho}$ for Equation (8.11)	$\hat{\rho}$ for Equation (8.12)
Overall	75	.70	.66
I	43	−.03	−.11
II	7	−.28	−.35
III	16	.36	.09
IV	9	.09	.05

The pattern of results for both regressions is similar. The estimated correlation coefficient for the overall test periods was strongly positive, but for the shorter periods, values are both smaller, and variable in sign, with the $+/-$ signs in agreement for the two equations. This suggests that the strongly indicated tendency toward positive serial correlation of the error term for the overall test period has been substantially reduced by separate consideration of subperiods, which were selected based upon their inventory ratio behavior.

Tables 39 and 40 also showed very different values of the coefficients estimated for the explanatory variables for the overall test period, and for the subperiods. We might infer from this that the various combinations of parameter coefficients yield an appreciable reduction of the tendency initially found for serial correlation of the error term. However, the assurance with which conclusions may be drawn from these observations has been weakened by the small number of observations in three of the four periods, which in turn has reduced the discriminatory power of the D-W test.

Next, the critical d_U and d_L values for the D-W statistic at the 5 percent and 1 percent levels of significance for the various test periods, and the conclusions drawn from the test statistics reported are shown on table 42. (note that the appropriate figure when $d^* < 2$ is $(4 - 3)$, of course.)

The following observations may be made on table 42:

1. For subperiods II and IV, each of which have less than fifteen observations, meaningful values for d_U and d_L are not available.

2. The very wide range between d_U and d_L for subperiod III (with sixteen observations) necessarily heavily favors the rather unhelpful test conclusion of "inconclusive." (In fact, for five variables and less than twenty observations, a null hypothesis result is literally not possible; and at the 1 percent level, a positive autocorrelation signal would require $d^* <$ .44, which is lower than *any* D-W result encountered in the study.)

Table 42. Durbin-Watson Test Statistics and Interpretation, from Regression Results on Equations (8.11) and (8.12) for Industry 28 for the Period 1958-1976 and Four Subdivisions of the Overall Period, QFR and BuCensus Quarterly Data, Nonseasonally Adjusted

No. of Obs.	For Equation (8.11)						For Equation (8.12)					
	d^*	@ 5%		@ 1%		Conclusion	d^*	@ 5%		@ 1%		Conclusion
		d_L	d_U	d_L	d_U			d_L	d_U	d_L	d_U	
75	.5913	1.57	1.68	1.42	1.53	positive autocorrelation	.6774	1.51	1.77	1.34	1.62	positive autocorrelation
43	2.0576	1.41	1.61	1.22	1.41	null hypothesis accepted	2.2207	1.27	1.78	1.09	1.58	indecisive @ 5% null hypoth. 1%
7	2.5699	-	-	-	-	-	2.707	-	-	-	-	-
16	1.2835	.98	1.54	.74	1.25	indecisive @ 5% null hypoth. 1%	1.820	.62	2.15	.44	1.90	indecisive 1-5%
9	1.8152	-	-	-	-	-	1.909	-	-	-	-	-

3. For a two variable regression with sixteen observations, the very low d_u of 1.25 (at 1 percent) requires acceptance of the null hypothesis (i.e., no autocorrelation) at the almost suspiciously low test d* value of 1.28.

4. This leaves open for useful consideration only the results for subperiod I (forty-three observations)—and here the conclusion of no autocorrelation of the error term seems clearly justified.

All this brings us back, of course, to the question, "Is autocollinearity present, and with what consequences?" One of the frequently encountered results of serial correlation of the error term is substantial understatement of error terms for the estimates of coefficients of the explanatory variables. Certainly, the period-to-period variability of the estimated coefficients (of tables 39 and 40) is well in excess of the standard errors reported, and this supports the suspicion that autocollinearity and its effects are indeed present.

Progress has been made, however. It has been demonstrated that no autocorrelation of the error term is found in period I (forty-three observations), and, at least, no conclusive evidence for it in period III (sixteen observations), and the two subperiods together comprise 80 percent of the overall test period. Nor does it appear likely that the strong positive autocorrelation displayed in the results for the overall period should be attributed to the two shorter subperiods II and IV—neither from their proportionately smaller weight nor the test results obtained for them. Instead, the presence (or absence) of autocollinearity appears highly dependent on the "choice" of parameter coefficients. Whether the variability displayed by these depends chiefly on factors reflected by inventory ratio behavior (which, after all, was the basis for selection of the subperiods), or on the strongly multicollinear tendencies previously analyzed, has not been determined. But since the latter factor has clearly affected parameter estimates, and these in turn seem directly related to the judgment made on autocollinearity, it would not seem unfair to relate the effects of multicollinearity.

Cochrane-Orcutt Test Results

The Cochrane-Orcutt iterative procedure produces an estimate of ρ through a series of OLSQ regressions in which the original data are "progressively transformed." To illustrate the scheme, the first round estimate, $\hat{\rho}$, of the autocorrelation coefficient is obtained by evaluation of the residual terms.

A second OLSQ regression is performed using the "transformed" relation:

$$(Y_t - \hat{\rho}Y_{t-1}) = b_0(1 - \hat{\rho}) + b_1(X_t - \hat{\rho}X_{t-1})$$
$$+ (u_t - \hat{\rho}u_{t-1})$$

which produces a second-round autocorrelation coefficient estimate, $\hat{\rho}$; this in turn is used for another transformation of data and another OLSQ regression. Et sequitur, until it may be fairly judged that the final round ρ estimate has converged.

Application of this technique produces the estimates tabulated for ρ (table 43).

The estimates for the overall test period value of ρ, for the two regression relates, agree well. The patterns are not as consistent for the subperiods. However, neither set of estimates of ρ for the subperiods appear to support the notion of an overall pattern (for the whole test period) of strongly marked positive autocollinearity. We would conclude at this point that the Cochrane-Orcutt results tend to confirm the observations made in the previous section.

Table 43. Cochrane-Orcutt Estimates of the Value of the
Autocorrelation Coefficient for Industry 28 from Equations (8.11) and
(8.12), for the Period 1958-1976 and Four Subdivisions of the Overall
Period, QFR and BuCensus Quarterly Data, Nonseasonally Adjusted

No. of Obs.	For Equation (8.11)				For Equation (8.12)			
	Final Value, ρ	No. of Iterations	Std. Error of ρ	$\underline{t}$ stat. for ρ	Final Value, ρ	No. of Iterations	Std. Error of ρ	$\underline{t}$ stat. for ρ
75	.816	4	.067	12.13	.803	3	.068	11.58
43	-.054	1	.154	-.348	-.463	6	.137	-3.38
7	-1.34	3	-	-	-1.151	5	-	-
16	.945	14	.085	11.16	.091	2	.257	.355
9	.042	4	.353	.119	-.763	11	.229	-3.39

Notes

Chapter 1

1. Armen A. Alchian, "Costs and Outputs," in *The Allocation of Economic Resources: Essays in Honor of Bernard F. Haley,* eds. M. Abramovitz et al. (Stanford, Cal.: Stanford University Press, 1959); reprinted in *Readings in Microeconomics* (2d ed.), eds. William Breit and Harold M. Hochman (New York: Holt, Rinehart, & Winston, 1971), pp. 159–71.

2. James Tobin, "Keynsian Models of Recession and Depression," *American Economic Review* 65 (May 1975).

3. John Maynard Keynes, *General Theory of Employment, Interest, and Money* (London: Macmillan Press, 1936), p. 51.

4. Observance of the second order condition that

$$\frac{d^2 C}{dq^2} > 0$$

for equation (1.1) is necessary, and its counterpart for relations (1.2)–(1.4), as well.

5. For derivation of these relations, including the second order convexity requirements, see James M. Henderson and Richard E. Quandt, *Microeconomic Theory: A Mathematical Approach (2d ed.) (New York: McGraw-Hill, 1971), pp. 63–97.*

6. ... by the assumptions underlying perfect competition, *certainty,* in particular.

7. Eli W. Clemens, "Price Discrimination and the Multiple-Product Firm," *The Review of Economic Studies* 19 (1951–1952): 1. Clemens reports, "Multiple-product production is universal and may be carried to extreme lengths." (examples cited.)

8. Herbert A. Simon, "Theories of Decision-Making in Economics," *American Economic Review* 49 (June 1959). Simon has coined the word "satisficing" to denote acceptance of satisfactory rates of return by managers, instead of true profit-maximizing. Jones' strategy could be interpreted as an example of this behavior.

9. Paul L. Joskow, "Firm Decision Making Processes and Oligopoly Theory," *American Economic Review* 65 (May 1975): 276.

Chapter 2

1. G. Ramsay, *An Essay on the Distribution of Wealth* (Edinburgh: Black, 1836), pp. 33–34.

2.   John Stuart Mill, *Essays on Some Unsettled Questions of Political Economy* (2d ed.) (London: Reader & Dyer, 1874), p. 67.

3.   John Bates Clark, *The Distribution of Wealth. A Theory of Wages, Interest, and Profits* (London: Macmillan Press, 1900), p. 14.

4.   Michael K. Evans, *Macroeconomic Activity: Theory, Forecasting and Control: An Econometric Approach* (New York: Harper & Row, 1969), p. 201.

5.   Keynes, *General Theory of Employment, Interest, and Money.*

6.   Ibid., pp. 215–18.

7.   Ibid., pp. 317–19.

8.   Ibid., p. 322.

9.   P.M. Sweezy, "Demand Under Conditions of Oligopoly," *Journal of Political Economy* 47 (August 1939).

10.   Thomson M. Whitin, *The Theory of Inventory Management* (2d ed.) (Princeton, N.J.: Princeton University Press, 1957).

11.   Franco Modigliani, "Business Reasons for Holding Inventories and Their Macro-economic Implications," in *Conference on Research in Income and Wealth: Studies in Income and Wealth* (Vol. 19) (New York: National Bureau of Economic Research, 1957).

12.   Vernon Smith, *Investment and Production* (Cambridge, Mass.: Harvard University Press, 1961).

13.   Marc Nerlove, "Lags in Economic Behaviour," *Econometrica* 40 (March 1972): 228.

14.   E.S. Phelps et al., *Microeconomic Foundations of Employment and Inflation Theory* (New York: W.W. Norton & Co., 1970). The term new microeconomics comes from the introduction to this book, but Nerlove makes a case for progress in this front even before then.

15.   Edwin S. Mills, "The Theory of Inventory Decisions," *Econometrica* 25 (April 1957).

16.   David P. Baron, "Demand Uncertainty in Imperfect Competition," *International Economic Review* 12 (June 1971).

17.   Hayne E. Leland, "Theory of the Firm Facing Uncertain Demand," *American Economic Review* 62 (June 1972).

18.   Duncan M. Holthausen, "Input Choices and Uncertain Demand," *American Economic Review* 66 (March 1976).

19.   David de Meza and Thomas van Ungern Sternberg, "Market Structure and Optimal Stockholding: A Note," *Journal of Political Economy* 88 (April 1980).

20.   Louis de Alessi, "The Short Run Revisited," *American Economic Review* 37 (June 1967): 153. Reprinted in William Breit and Harold M. Hochman (eds.), *Readings in Microeconomics* (2d ed.) (New York: Holt, Rinehart, & Winston, 1971).

21.   Richard E. Caves et al., "Competitive Conditions and the Firm's Buffer Stocks: An Exploratory Analysis," *Review of Economics and Statistics* 61 (November 1979).

22.   Mill, *Essays on Some Unsettled Questions of Political Economy,* p. 55.

23.   For development of the concept, see David E.W. Laidler, *The Demand for Money: Theories and Evidence* (2d ed.) (New York: Dun-Donnelly, 1977).

24. Henderson and Quandt, *Microeconomic Theory: A Mathematical Approach*, p. 99.

25. A useful summary of econometric studies dealing with inventory investment is given in Evans, *Macroeconomic Activity*, pp. 201-20.

26. Lloyd A. Metzler, "The Nature and Stability of Inventory Cycles," *Review of Economics and Statistics* 23 (August 1941).

27. Evans, *Macroeconomic Activity*, pp. 377–78. On the basis that manufacturers' and distributors' postwar inventories have averaged ~ forty-fifty days of sales, Evans' test of Metzler's equation, using a one-quarter lag, produces "a reasonable solution."

28. Thomson M. Whitin, "Inventory Control Research: A Survey," *Management Science 1* (October 1954): 33.

29. The point is developed by Paul Davidson, *Money and the Real World* (New York: Wiley, 1972), p. 49, n. 4.

30. Lawrence E. Klein and Joel Popkin, "An Econometric Analysis of the Postwar Relationship Between Inventory Fluctuations and Changes in Aggregate Economic Activity," in *Inventory Fluctuations and Economic Stabilization*, Part III (Washington: Joint Economic Committee of the U.S. 87th Congress, 1961).

31. Paul G. Darling, "Manufacturers' Inventory Investment, 1947–1958: An Application of Acceleration Analysis," *American Economic Review* 49 (December 1959).

32. Michael E. Lovell, "Manufacturers' Inventories, Sales Expectations, and the Acceleration Principle," *Econometrica* 29 (July 1961).

33. Ibid.

34. Paul G. Darling, "Inventory Fluctuations and Economic Instability: An Analysis Based on the Postwar Economy," in *Inventory Fluctuations and Economic Stabilization*, Part III (Washington: Joint Economic Committee of the U.S. 87th Congress, 1st Session, 1961).

35. B. Peter Pashigian, "The Relevance of Sales Anticipatory Data in Explaining Inventory Investment," *International Economic Review* 6 (January 1965).

36. A.A. Hirsch and Michael Lovell, *Sales Anticipations and Inventory Behaviour* (New York: John C. Wiley & Sons, 1969).

37. Thomas M. Stanback, Jr., "Postwar Cycles in Manufacturers' Inventories," in *Inventory Fluctuations and Economic Stabilization*, Part I (Washington: Joint Economic Committee of the 87th Congress, 1961).

38. Ruth P. Mack, "Changes in Ownership of Purchased Materials," in *Inventory Fluctuations and Economic Stabilization*, Part II (Washington: Joint Economic Committee of the U.S. 87th Congress, 1961); and *Information, Expectations, and Inventory Fluctuations: A Study of Materials Stock on Hand and on Order* (New York: National Bureau of Economic Research, Columbia University Press, 1967).

39. Moses Abramovitz, *Inventories and Business Cycles with Special Reference to Manufacturers' Inventories* (New York: National Bureau of Economic Research, 1950).

40. U.S. Congress, 1967, p. 6.

41. Klein and Popkin, "An Econometric Analysis of the Postwar Relationship Between Inventory Fluctuations and Changes in Aggregate Economic Activity," pp. 71–86.

42. The Joint Economic Committee of the 87th Congress deserves special mention as a heavyweight team. Its membership included Senators Paul Douglas (coauthor of Cobb-

Douglas), William Proxmire, Prescott Bush, and Edmund Fulbright; Representatives Wright Patman, Henry Reus, and Martha Griffiths.

43.   Holt et al., *Planning Production, Inventories and Work Force* (Englewood Cliffs, N.J.: Prentice-Hall, 1960).

44.   Charles Holt and Franco Modigliani, "Firm Cost Structures and the Dynamic Responses of Inventories, Production, Work Force, and Orders to Sales Fluctuations," in *Inventory Fluctuations and Economic Stabilization,* Part II (Washington: Joint Economic Committee of the U.S. 87th Congress, 1961).

45.   David A. Belsley, *Industry Production Behaviour: The Order-Stock Distinction* (Amsterdam: North-Holland Publishing Co., 1969).

46.   A contemporary study by Belsley's colleague, Childs, deserves similar recognition for this improved approach. Gerald L. Childs, *Unfilled Orders and Inventories: A Structural Analysis.* (Amsterdam: North-Holland Publishing Co., 1967).

47.   Andrew Z. Szendrovitz, "Manufacturing Cycle Time Determination for a Multi-Stage Economic Production Quantity Model," *Management Sciences* 21 (November 1975).

48.   Reference to number 7, chapter 1.

49.   Salah E. Elmaghraby, "The Economic Lot Scheduling Problem (ELSP): Review and Extensions," *Management Science* 24 (February 1978).

50.   J.F. Williams, "Multi-Echelon Production Scheduling when Demand is Stochastic," *Management Science* 20 (1974): 1253–63.

51.   W. Crowston et al., "Economic Lot Size Determination in Multi-Stage Assembly Systems," *Management Science* 19 (1973): 517–27.

52.   As an example, R.R. Vemuganti, "On the Feasibility of Scheduling Lot Sizes for Two Products on One Machine," *Management Science* 24 (November 1978).

53.   As an example, C.L. Doll and D.C. Whybark, "An Iterative Procedure for the Single-Machine, Multiple Product Lot Scheduling Problem," *Management Science* 20 (1973): 50–55.

54.   Harvey M. Wagner, "Research Portfolio for Inventory Management and Production Planning Systems," *Operations Research* 28 (1980): 447.

55.   For a recent review of MRP research articles, see Wagner, "Research Portfolio," p. 453.

56.   A.M. Geoffrion, "Better Distribution Planning with Computer Models," *Harvard Business Review* 52 (July-August 1976).

57.   M. Oral et al., "On the Evaluation of Shortage Costs for Inventory Control of Finished Goods," *Management Science* 18 (1972): B344–B351.

58.   Wagner, "Research Portfolio."

Chapter 3

1.   I.e., MC = P, or its multi-product analogs.

2.   Holt et al., *Planning Production, Inventories and Work Force.*

3.   Holt and Modigliani, "Firm Cost Structures."

4. Mills, "The Theory of Inventory Decisions," assumed stochastic demand, the firm as a price setter; and he is at pains to demonstrate, in tems of maximized present value, that the cost-minimizing solution is also profit-maximizing.

5. Other segments of the managerial data base include: personnel and labor relations, process technology and product development, supplies and services, condition of equipment and facilities, and resolution of specific short-term technical and marketing problems.

6. Both in the making of this point, and, in fact, the approach used to illustrate it, this study has followed Belsley's example. Belsley, "Industry Production Behaviour: The Order Stock Distinction."

Chapter 4

1. Abramovitz, *Inventories and Business Cycles with Special Reference to Manufacturers' Inventories.*

2. Mack, *Information, Expectations, and Inventory Fluctuations.*

3. Victor Zarnowitz, *Unfilled Orders, Price Changes and Business Fluctuations,* NBER Occasional Paper 84 (New York: National Bureau of Economic Research, 1962).

4. Stanback, "Postwar Cycles in Manufacturers' Inventories."

5. Darling, "Manufacturers' Inventory Investment, 1947–1958," and "Inventory Fluctuations and Economic Instability."

6. Lovell, "Manufacturers' Inventories, Sales Expectations, and the Acceleration Principle;" Michael C. Lovell, "Sales Anticipations, Planned Inventory Investment, and Realizations," in *Determinants of Investment Behavior,* ed. Robert Ferber (New York: National Bureau of Economic Research, 1967).

7. Klein and Popkin, "An Econometric Analysis of the Postwar Relationship Between Inventory Fluctuations and Changes in Aggregate Economic Activity."

8. E.g., as in the Wharton EFU model, equation (15.8). See Evans, *Macroeconomic Activity,* pp. 219, 220, 434.

9. Belsley, *Industry Production Behaviour.* A contemporary study by Belsley's colleague, Childs, *Unfilled Orders and Inventories,* deserves similar recognition as a contribution in this area.

10. Exceptions may occur during periods of abnormal shortage, periods of rationing, etc.

11. Childs, *Unfilled Orders and Inventories,* p. 5.

12. E.g., the typical "job shop" in the printing or fabricated metals industries.

13. Childs observes, "In the United States, most manufacturers produce *both* to order and to stock. For products which are made to order, raw material and inprocess inventories are relatively high, finished goods stocks low, backlogs high. For products made to stock the opposite is typical under normal circumstances. It might therefore be safe to infer that for a firm which produces both to order and to stock, backlogs would mostly be associated with made-to-order items, and finished good inventories are most significantly of items produced to stock," *Unfilled Orders and Inventories,* p. 4.

14. Lovell, "Manufacturers' Inventories, Sales Expectations, and the Acceleration Principle."

15. Hirsch and Lovell, *Sales Anticipations and Inventory Behaviour.*

16.   Pashigian, "The Relevance of Sales Anticipatory Data in Explaining Inventory Investment."

17.   Belsley, *Industry Production Behaviour,* pp. 65, 66.

18.   Ibid., pp. 67, 68.

19.   In fact, for the sake of continuity, we might just as well peek now at the results obtained from regression tests on quarterly, nonseasonally adjusted data (as before) for the five industries of this study in which manufacture *both* to stock and to order is common. The sums of coefficients d_2 and d_6 for industries 26, 27, 34, 35, and 36 respectively were: .057, .059, −.010, −.022, and .101. The mean of these sums is .037, which is reasonably in the spirit of the assumptions made. However the standard deviation (.052) is twice as large as that for the sums of the $d_1 + d_3$ coefficients given on p. 101. For the latter, $X = 1.061$ and $s = .052$.

20.   Or, more correctly, a $m \cdot \mu_t^s$ term, with $m = 1$.

21.   The error term has been modified by the addition of ϵ_t to: $v_t = w_t + \epsilon_t$.

Chapter 5

1.   Three of the sixteen Durbin-Watson test statistics were 2.11−2.35, which would be equivalent to $(4\text{-}d^*) = 1.65\text{–}1.89$. The remainder were 1.12−1.97.

2.   A. Koutsoyiannis, *Theory of Econometrics* (2d ed.) (New York: Harper & Row, Barnes & Noble Import Dvision, 1978), p. 226.

3.   Zvi Griliches, "A Note on the Serial Correlation Bias in Estimates of Distributed Lags," *Econometrica* 29 (1961): 65–73.

4.   Mark Nerlove and K. Wallis, "Use of the Durbin-Watson Statistic in Inappropriate Situations," *Econometrica* 34 (1966): 235–38.

5.   Koutsoyiannis, *Theory of Econometrics,* p. 309.

6.   The remainder of this paragraph follows the (very clear) exposition of Judge et al., *The Theory and Practice of Econometrics* (New York: John Wiley & Sons, 1980).

7.   Reminder is appropriate that the model has *not* been presented as a simple linear decision rule which managers could use to quickly calculate optimal production rates—that would be putting the cart before the horse. The purpose of these tests is to see if production decisions have been made on a profit-maximizing basis.

8.   In a sense, this simply restates the basic production to stock relation:

$$P_t^s = S_t^s + \Delta H_t$$

says that current output is either sold during the period, or added to the stock of finished goods.

9.   Two additional rationales are provided by Belsley, *Industry Production Behaviour:* (a) a period is assumed to be defined "in some natural way" by the production process. The length of period is *not* assumed arbitrarily to be a week, a month, or a quarter (pp. 9, 10); (b) rigorous derivation of (5.1) requires that the sales expectations term represent a weighted average vector of forward expectations over the firm's time horizon—an assumption later relaxed. However, simplification of this term to $d_3\mu_t$ would also affect the relative values of d_2 and d_3 (pp. 19–43).

10. Arnold Zellner and Claude Montmarquette, "A Study of Some Aspects of Temporal Aggregation Problems in Econometric Analysis," *Review of Economics and Statistics* 55 (August 1973).

11. The ratio of d_2 (quarterly)/d_2 monthly for Industries 20, 21, and 29 respectively were 3.08, 1.85, and 3.64.

12. Belsley, *Industry Production Behaviour,* pp. 16–68.

13. "Compete" is being used here metaphorically rather than literally. Goods, of course, do not compete, but it *is* a constant part of the manager's responsibility to decide which should receive preference.

14. "Brisk" and "slack" have a pleasantly old-fashioned ring, don't they? In fact they were terms employed by one of the earlier writers on this very subject. Mill, *Essays on Some Unsettled Questions of Political Economy.*

Chapter 6

1. Asset management ratios are conventionally presented in terms of a 360-day year—and this convention is followed here. Eugene F. Brigham, *Fundamentals of Financial Management* (2d ed.) (Hinsdale, Ill.: Dryden Press, 1980), pp. 152–59.

2. Moody's Investors Service, *Moody's Industrial Survey* (annual) (New York: 1977).

3. The "for want of a nail the shoe was lost; for want of a shoe the horse . . . " case.

4. R.J. Campbell and T.M. Porcano, "Improving Inventory Control Through Data Base Concepts," *Management Accounting* (January 1979).

5. Jay Severance and R.R. Bottin, "Work-in-process Inventory Control Through Data Base Concepts," *Management Accounting* (January 1979).

6. Since work-in-process represents, by definition, *incomplete work,* it follows that additional work and/or additional raw materials or components are required to produce saleable product(s). The purpose of the 75 percent figure is to illustrate this point, rather than to precisely fix the actual figure.

7. Quarterly sales, S_t, which are not included in table 19, correlate very closely with P_t. The correlation coefficients for the four industries are: .9995, .9943, .9997, and .9999 respectively.

8. These particular figures represent ratios of finished goods to quarterly sales two times greater than the mean for the period, and as much as four times larger than individual earlier values— in other words, a substantial upward shift has occurred.

9. Whitin, "Inventory Control Research."

10. Under the usual small-sample test assumptions, particularly that both sampled populations have approximately normal distributions.

11. James M. Griffin, "The Process Analysis Alternative to Statistical Cost Functions: An Application to Petroleum Refining," *American Economic Review* 42 (March 1972).

12. A more complete model would probably include other potential short-term financing needs, such as other forms of inventories held and receivables. With regard to form of the expression, a logarithmic function, which would allow demonstration of proportionalities might well offer promise.

Chapter 7

1. Evans, *Macroeconomic Activity,* p. 207.

2. It bears note that the large part of manufacturers' output is sold to other firms, frequently on either a regular or a contractual basis. Reference to Leontiev's Input-Output tables demonstrates the point.

3. The reminder is appropriate that, because of identity (7.1), the values of e_t in (7.6) and (7.5) are identical.

4. The number of months required for a coefficient of *one* is also, of course, a function of the growth rate of the industry.

5. BuCensus figures are reported in current dollars, not real dollars. The nine percent growth referred to is, therefore, in terms of current dollars, and not real growth.

6. Standard deviations of greater utility would be derived by using the "trend line" technique. This suggests yet another approach, the use of regression analysis, which is employed further below.

7. Summarizing the results of the regression test of:

    $$H_t = a + b \cdot S_t + \epsilon_t,$$

    as has been done in table 31, facilitates comparison, but necessarily omits some useful data. To enable the reader to better weigh the results, data on the R^2's of the regressions is given here:

Range of $\bar{R}^2$	Industry 20	Industry 21	Industry 28	Industry 29
Highest	.9733	.8776	.9587	.9815
Lowest	.9414	.6595	.8977	.9069
Mean	.9614	.7556	.9287	.9492

8. Evans, *Macroeconomic Activity,* pp. 202–04.

9. Darling, "Manufacturers" Inventory Investment," p. 23.

10. Smith, *Investment and Production.*

11. In a simple case with uniform marginal cost per unit, longer production runs would minimize annual production costs by incurring fewer setup charges per year. However, fewer but larger runs would mean a larger average product inventory, and hence higher inventory carrying costs.

    The familiar square root relation developed by Whitin can be derived as the solution (i.e., economic lot size) for this example by equating inventory carrying costs and setup costs, and solving for the quantity involved. (Whitin, "Inventory Control Research."

12. The assumption has been chosen as representing the most general case. It is true that higher setup costs for an individual product could result in its being produced at lower frequency (i.e., not being produced each cycle). At the extreme, the product would be produced to order, not stock.

    On the other hand, if the typical product could be economically produced at multiple times during the production cycle, the length of the cycle has, ipso facto, been misspecified.

13. The others: setup and/or changeover costs (including time involved), inventory costs, and opportunity costs. We assume, by inclusion of opportunity costs, that P_1 is a product of adequate profitability to merit inclusion in the schedule.

14. It is implicit in this relation that sales of any units of this product during its period of manufacture are drawn from $q_{-1,i}$ (i.e., the amount of the i'th product made in the previous production cycle in anticipation of near term sales).

15. Frequently, in the econometric literature, reference is made to "manufacturers' decisions on inventory investment." The phraseology is probably due to the relation:

$$Y = C + I + G,$$

and the importance of changes in investments in inventory in macroeconomic forecasting studies. However, the point being made here is that changes in inventory investment are the direct result of the *production decisions* of manufacturers.

Chapter 8

1. de Alessi, "The Short Run Revisited."

2. Holt and Modigliani, "Firm Cost Structures."

3. Other examples can be given. Another would be: a firm collecting what its customers owe it (i.e., receivables) would reduce the latter, and increase cash correspondingly. The noncollecting firm, and the collecting one, would still show the same total current assets.

4. D.E. Farrar and R.R. Glauber, "Multicollinearity in Regression Analysis; the Problem Revisited," *Review of Economics and Statistics* 49 (1967).

5. Data for Industry 28, originally given on tables 37 and 38, is repeated on tables 39 and 40, *plus* the test results for four subperiods of the overall test period.

6. Judge et al., *The Theory and Practice of Econometrics,* pp. 460–61.

7. Koutsoyiannis, *Theory of Econometrics,* pp. 226, 227.

Bibliography

Abramovitz, Moses. *Inventories and Business Cycles with Special Reference to Manufacturers' Inventories.* New York: National Bureau of Economic Research, 1950.

Alchian, Armen A. "The Basis of Some Recent Advances in the Theory of Management of the Firm." *Journal of Industrial Economics* 14 (November 1965). Rpt. In William Breit and Harold M. Hochman, eds. *Readings in Microeconomics.* 2d ed. New York: Holt, Rinehart, & Winston, 1971, pp. 131–39.

_____. "Costs and Outputs." In *The Allocation of Economic Resources: Essays in Honor of Bernard F. Haley.* M. Abramovitz. Stanford, Cal.: Stanford University Press, 1959. Rpt. in William Breit and Harold M. Hochman, eds. *Readings in Microeconomics.* 2d ed. New York: Holt, Rinehart, & Winston, 1971, pp. 159–71.

Baron, David P. "Demand Uncertainty in Imperfect Competition." *International Economic Review* 12 (June 1971).

Baumol, William J. *Economic Theory and Operations Analysis.* 2d ed. Englewood Cliffs, N.J.: Prentice-Hall, 1965.

Belsley, David A. *Industry Production Behaviour: The Order-Stock Distinction.* Amsterdam: North-Holland Publishing Co., 1969.

Breit, William, and Hochman, Harold M., eds. *Readings in Microeconomics.* 2d ed. New York: Holt, Rinehart, & Winston, 1971.

Brigham, Eugene F. *Fundamentals of Financial Management.* 2d ed. Hinsdale, Ill.: Dryden Press, 1980.

Business Week. "Inventories May Be a Drag Again," 5 December 1977, p. 30.

Campbell, R.J., and Porcano, T.M. "Improving Inventory Control with Materials Requirements Planning." *Cost and Management* (January 1979).

Caves, Richard E.; Jarret, J. Peter; and Loucks, Michael K. "Competitive Conditions and the Firm's Buffer Stocks: An Exploratory Analysis." *Review of Economics and Statistics* 61 (November 1979).

Childs, Gerald L. *Unfilled Orders and Inventories: A Structural Analysis.* Amsterdam: North-Holland Publishing Co., 1967.

_____. "Inventories and the Generalized Accelerator." In *Trade, Stability, and Macroeconomics: Essays in Honor of Lloyd A. Metzler.* New York: Academic Press, 1974.

Clark, John Bates. *The Distribution of Wealth. (A Theory of Wages, Interest, and Profits.)* London: Macmillan Press, 1900.

Clemens, Eli W. "Price Discrimination and the Multiple-Product Firm." *The Review of Economic Studies* 19 (1951–1952).

Crowston, W.; Wagner, M.; and Williams, J.F. "Economic Lot Size Determination in Multi-Stage Assembly Systems." *Management Science* 19 (1973): 517–27.

Darling, Paul G. "Manufacturers' Inventory Investment, 1947–1958: An Application of Acceleration Analysis." *American Economic Review* 49 (December 1959).

_____. "Inventory Fluctuations and Economic Instability: An Analysis Based on the Postwar Economy." In *Inventory Fluctuations and Economic Stabilization, Part III*. Washington: Joint Economic Committee of the U.S. 87th Congress, 1st Session, 1961.

_____, and Lovell, Michael C. "Inventories, Production-Smoothing and the Flexible Accelerator." *Quarterly Journal of Economics* 85 (May 1971).

Davidson, Paul. *Money and the Real World*. New York: Wiley, 1972.

de Alessi, Louis. "The Short Run Revisited." *American Economic Review* 37 (June 1967). Rpt. in William Breit and Harold M. Hochman, eds. *Readings in Microeconomics*. 2d ed. New York: Holt, Rinehart, & Winston, 1971, pp. 149–58.

de Meza, David, and Sternberg, Thomas von Ungern. "Market Structure and Optimal Stockholding: A Note." *Journal of Political Economy* 88 (April 1980).

Doll, C.L., and Whybark, D.C. "An Iterative Procedure for the Single-Machine, Multiple Product Lot Scheduling Problem." *Management Science* 20 (1973): 50–55.

Elmaghraby, Salah E. "The Economic Lot Scheduling Problem (ELSP): Review and Extensions." *Management Science* 24 (February 1978).

Evans, Michael K. *Macroeconomic Activity: Theory, Forecasting and Control: An Econometric Approach*. New York: Harper & Row, 1969.

Federal Trade Commission. "Quarterly Financial Report on Manufacturing Industries." Washington, D.C.: Division of Financial Statistics, Federal Trade Commission, quarterly.

Geoffrion, A.M. "Better Distribution Planning with Computer Models." *Harvard Business Review* 52 (July-August 1976).

Griffin, James M. "The Process Analysis Alternative to Statistical Cost Functions: An Application to Petroleum Refining." *American Economic Review* 42 (March 1972).

Griliches Zvi. "A Note on the Serial Correlation Bias in Estimates of Distributed Lags." *Econometrica* 29 (1961): 65–73.

Hay, George A. "Adjustment Costs and the Flexible Accelerator." *Quarterly Journal of Economics* 84 (February 1970): 140–43.

_____. "Production, Price, and Inventory Theory." *American Economic Review* 60 (September 1970).

Henderson, James M., and Quandt, Richard E. *Microeconomic Theory: A Mathematical Approach*. 2d ed. New York: McGraw-Hill, 1971.

Hirsch, A.A., and Lovell, Michael. *Sales Anticipations and Inventory Behaviour*. New York: John C. Wiley & Sons, 1969.

Holt, Charles, and Modigliani, Franco. "Firm Cost Structures and the Dynamic Responses of Inventories, Production, Work Force, and Orders to Sales Fluctuations." In *Inventory Fluctuations and Economic Stabilization, Part II*. Washington, D.C.: Joint Economic Committee of the U.S. 87th Congress, 1961.

_____, Modigliani, Franco; Muth, John F.; and Simon, Herbert A. *Planning Production, Inventories and Work Force*. Englewood Cliffs, N.J.: Prentice-Hall, 1960.

Holthausen, Duncan M. "Input Choices and Uncertain Demand." *American Economic Review* 66 (March 1976).

Joskow, Paul L. "Firm Decision Making Processes and Oligopoly Theory." *American Economic Review* 65 (May 1975).

Judge, George G.; Griffiths, William E.; Hill, R. Carter; and Lee, Tsoung-Chao. *The Theory and Practice of Econometrics*. New York: John Wiley & Sons, 1980.

Kaufman, George G. *The U.S. Financial System: Money, Markets and Institutions*. Englewood Cliffs, N.J.: Prentice-Hall, 1980.

Keynes, John Maynard. *General Theory of Employment, Interest, and Money*. London: Macmillan Press, 1936.

Klein, Lawrence E., and Popkin, Joel. "An Econometric Analysis of the Postwar Relationship Between Inventory Fluctuations and Changes in Aggregate Economic Activity." In *Inventory*

Fluctuations and Economic Stabilization, Part III. Washington, D.C.: Joint Economic Committee of the U.S. 87th Congress, 1961.

Koutsoyiannis, A. *Theory of Econometrics.* 2d ed. New York: Harper & Row, Barnes & Noble Import Division, 1978.

Laidler, David E.W. *The Demand for Money: Theories and Evidence.* 2nd ed. New York: Dun-Donnelly, 1977.

Leland, Hayne E. "Theory of the Firm Facing Uncertain Demand." *American Economic Review* 62 (June 1972).

Lovell, Michael C. "Manufacturers' Inventories, Sales Expectations, and the Acceleration Principle." *Econometrica* 29 (July 1961).

————. "Sales Anticipations, Planned Inventory Investment, and Realization." In *Determinants of Investment Behavior.* Edited by Robert Ferber. New York: National Bureau of Economic Research, 1967.

Mack, Ruth P. "Changes in Ownership of Purchased Materials." In *Inventory Fluctuations and Economic Stabilization, Part II.* Washington, D.C.: Joint Economic Committee of the U.S. 87th Congress, 1961.

————. *Information, Expectations, and Inventory Fluctuations: A Study of Materials Stock on Hand and on Order.* New York: National Bureau of Economic Research, Columbia University Press, 1967.

Metzler, Lloyd A. "The Nature and Stability of Inventory Cycles." *Review of Economics and Statistics* 23 (August 1941).

Mill, John Stuart. *Essays on Some Unsettled Questions of Political Economy.* 2d ed. London: Reader & Dyer, 1874.

Mills, Edwin S. "The Theory of Inventory Decisions." *Econometrica* 25 (April 1957).

————. "Uncertainty and Price Theory." *Quarterly Journal of Economics* 73 (February 1959): 116.

————. *Price, Output, and Inventory Policy.* New York John Wiley & Sons, 1962.

Modigliani, Franco. "Business Reasons for Holding Inventories and Their Macro-economic Implications." In *Conference on Research in Income and Wealth: Studies in Income and Wealth.* Vol. 19. New York: National Bureau of Economic Research, 1957.

Moody's Investor Service. *Moody's Industrial Survey.* New York: 1977. (Annual.)

Nerlove, Marc. "Lags in Economic Behaviour." *Econometrica* 40 (March 1972).

————, and Wallis, K. "Use of the Durbin-Watson Statistic in Inappropriate Situations." *Econometrica* 34 (1966): 235–38.

Pashigian, B. Peter. "The Relevance of Sales Anticipatory Data in Explaining Inventory Investment." *International Economic Review* 6 (January 1965).

Phelps, E.S., et al. *Microeconomic Foundations of Employment and Inflation Theory.* New York: W.W. Norton & Co., 1970.

Quirk, James, and Saposnik, Rubin. *Introduction to General Equilibrium Theory and Welfare Economics.* New York: McGraw-Hill, 1968.

Ramsay, G. *An Essay on the Distribution of Wealth.* Edinburgh: Black, 1836.

Severance, Jay, and Bottin, R.R. "Work-in-process Inventory Control through Data Base Concepts." *Management Accounting* (January 1979).

Simon, Herbert A. "Theories of Decision-Making in Economics." *American Economic Review* 49 (June 1959).

Smith, Vernon. *Investment and Production.* Cambridge, Mass.: Harvard University Press, 1961.

Stanback, Thomas M., Jr. "Postwar Cycles in Manufacturers' Inventories." In *Inventory Fluctuations and Economic Stabilization, Part I.* Washington, D.C.: Joint Economic Committee of the 87th Congress, 1961.

Sweezy, P.M. "Demand Under Conditions of Oligopoly." *Journal of Political Economy* 47 (August 1939).

Szendrovitz, Andrew Z. "Manufacturing Cycle Time Determination for a Multi-Stage Economic Production Quantity Model." *Management Science* 21 (November 1975).

Tobin, James. "Keynesian Models of Recession and Depression." *American Economic Review* 65 (May 1975).

U.S. Bureau of the Census. *Manufacturers' Shipments, Inventories, and Orders: 1947–1976* (revised). Washington, D.C.: Government Printing Office, 1977.

U.S. Congress. Joint Economic Committee. *Hearings: Inventory Fluctuation and Economic Stabilization.* Washington, D.C.: 87th Congress, 2d session, GPO, 1962.

U.S. Federal Trade Commission. *Quarterly Financial Review: 1958–1976.* Washington, D.C.: Government Printing Office.

Vemuganti, R.R. "On the Feasibility of Scheduling Lot Sizes for Two Products on One Machine." *Management Science* 24 (November 1978).

Wagner, Harvey M. "Research Portfolio for Inventory Management and Production Planning Systems." *Operations Research* 28 (1980): 445–75.

Wall Street Journal. "Businesses Aim for Stricter Controls as Slump Exposes Inventory Bulge," 15 August 1980, p. 17, column 4.

Walters, A.A. "Production and Cost Functions: An Econometric Survey." *Econometrica* 31 (April 1963).

Weston, J. Fred. "A Generalized Uncertainty Theory of Profit." *American Economic Review* 40 (March 1950).

Whitin, Thomson M. "Inventory Control Research: A Survey." *Management Sciences* 1 (October 1954).

———. *The Theory of Inventory Management.* 2d ed. Princeton, N.J.: Princeton University Press, 1957.

Williams, J.F. "Multi-Echelon Production Scheduling When Demand is Stochastic." *Management Sciences* 20 (1974): 1253–63.

Zarnowitz, Victor. *Unfilled Orders, Price Changes and Business Flucutations.* NBER Occasional Paper. New York: National Bureau of Economic Research, 1962.

Zellner, Arnold and Montmarquette, Claude. "A Study of Some Aspects of Temporal Aggregation Problems in Econometric Analysis." *Review of Economics and Statistics* 55 (August 1973).

Index

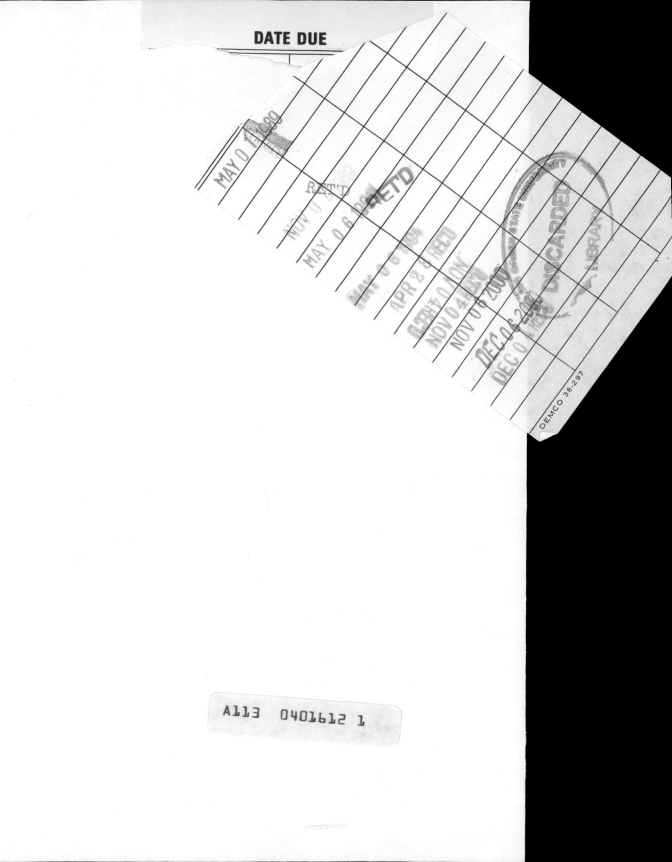